SUPER 21

A TREASURE TROVE

21 Taxalogues/Articles on
Income Tax, GST, PF, ESI, IBC
& Banking Regulation Act

Mayank Mohanka

{FCA, B.Com(Hons)SRCC}

ISBN 978-1-64828-317-8

Table of Contents

S. Nos.	Title Particulars	Page Nos.
1.	Cover Page	1
1.	Table of Contents	2-5
3.	Preface to the Book	6-9
4.	About the Author	10-11
5.	Taxalogue 1: Business Enterprises & Their Struggle through 'Indian Regulatory Framework'!!	12-29
6.	Taxalogue 2: Do You Think Tax Before Investing? Personal Investments & Income Tax	30-41
7.	Taxalogue 3: e-Assessment & e-Invoicing: Digital Transformation of Indian Tax Administration	42-83
8.	Taxalogue 4: Income & Expenditure pertaining to Pre-commencement of Business: Revenue or Capital?	84-101

9.	Taxalogue 5: Colourable Devices vs. GAAR	102-110
10.	Taxalogue 6: Going for a Date with Assessing Authority for Stay of Demand	111-116
11.	Taxalogue 7: Charitable Trusts: Income Tax Perspective	117-139
12.	Taxalogue 8: Tata's Six Charitable Trusts' Registration: Cancellation or Voluntary Surrender?	140-158
13.	Taxalogue 9: Joint Development Agreements: Income Tax Perspective	159-170
14.	Taxalogue 10: Are Sections 50C/43CA/56(2) of Income Tax Act Resulting in Double Taxation & Contrary to Real Income Theory?	171-181
15.	Taxalogue 11: Applicability of Section 56(2) on Fresh/Bonus/Right Issue &	182-187

	Buy Back of Shares: An Undying Conundrum!!	
16.	Taxalogue 12: Have Coercive Tax Recovery Measures Outlived their Utility?	188-196
17.	Taxalogue 13: Review of Existing Prosecution Provision u/s 276B	197-206
18.	Taxalogue 14: TDS on Power Transmission &Wheeling Charges u/s 194J/194I/194C of Income Tax Act	207-223
19.	Taxalogue 15: Commission Agents & Brokers: GST Perspective	224-244
20.	Taxalogue 16: Is GST Applicable on Naturopathy, Ayurveda, Yoga, Siddha, Unani & Homeopathy Based Medical Treatments?	245-248
21.	Taxalogue 17: GST Rate on Locomotive Engines Used	249-259

	Solely in Indian Railways: An Undying Conundrum!!	
22.	Taxalogue 18: Is SC Judgement holding Allowances as Part of Basic Wages for PF Contribution Contradictory?	260-272
23.	Taxalogue 19: ESI - Chinta se Mukti only till You Receive Notice u/s 45A of The ESI Act 1948	273-283
24.	Taxalogue 20: Rationalisation of IBC: A Lot Has Been Done...Still A Lot More Needs to be Done...	284-293
25.	Taxalogue 21: NBFCs: Impact Assessment of Carrot & Stick Approach of Amendments in Budget 2019-20	294-308
26.	Acknowledgement	309-310

Preface

The Book *"Super 21"* is a *'Treasure Trove'* of *'21'* distinguished, insightful, informative & practically useful 'Taxalogues/Articles' on *Indian Income-tax, GST, IBC, PF, ESI, Air & Water Pollution Acts & Banking/NBFC sector.*

These *'21 write-ups/gems crafted with precision'* are the culmination of *'21 Real-life Experiences'* showcasing the journey of the Business Enterprises through the Indian Regulatory Framework.

The Number '21' is considered 'auspicious' in our Indian Culture and as such the 21 precious Gems in the form of Taxalogues/Articles, encompassing Real-life Experiences, treasured in this Book, will surely serve as auspicious, handy and practically useful ready-references for the Entrepreneurs, Tax-Practitioners and Taxpayers in the day-to-day running of their diversified business/professional ventures amidst the taxing regulatory framework, in an effective, stress-free and seamless manner.

This Book is a 'Ready Referencer' for Entrepreneurs, Taxpayers & Tax Practitioners, in their Regulatory Compliances & Tax-Planning Pursuits and includes invaluable and practically oriented *'Taxalogues'* on *'21'* diversified issues/subjects having immense practical utility, including:

(i) Business Enterprises & their Struggle through the Regulatory Business Environment.

(ii) Do You Think Tax before Investing? Personal Investments & Income Tax.

(iii) Income & Expenditure pertaining to Pre-Commencement Business Period: Whether Revenue or Capital?

(iv) e-Assessments & e-Invoicing: Digital Transformation of Indian Tax Administration.

(v) Going for a Date with Assessing Authority for Stay of Demand.

(vi) Colourable Device vs. GAAR.

(vii) Taxability of Charitable Trusts.

(viii) Tata's Six Charitable Trust's Registration: Cancellation or Voluntary Surrender?

(ix) Taxability of Joint Development Agreements (JDAs).

(x) Sections 50C/43CA/56(2)(x) of Income-tax Act: Double Taxation?

(xi) Applicability of Section 56(2) on Fresh/Bonus/Right/Buy Back of Shares: An Undying Conundrum.

(xii) Have Conventional Coercive Tax Recovery Measures Outlived their Utility?

(xiii) Review of the Existing Prosecution Provision u/s 276B of the Income Tax Act, 1961- Need of the Hour is to Take Taxpayer Friendly Initiative.

(xiv) TDS on Power Transmission & Wheeling Charges u/s 194I/194J & 194C of Income Tax Act.

(xv) GST on Commission Agents & Brokers.

(xvi) GST Rate on Locomotive Engines Used Solely in Indian Railways: An Undying Conundrum.

(xvii) GST on Yoga, Naturopathy, Ayurveda, Yoga, Siddha, Unani & Homeopathy based Medical Treatments.

(xviii) Is SC Judgement holding Allowances as part of Basic Wages for PF Contribution Contradictory?

(xix) ESI – 'Chinta se Mukti' only till You Receive Notice u/s 45A of The ESI Act 1948.

(xx) Rationalisation of IBC: A Lot More Needs to be Done.

(xxi) NBFCs: Impact Assessment of Carrot & Stick Approach of Amendments in Union Budget 2019-20.

This Book characterizes a *'natural blend of law and practice'* concerning the *'Indian Regulatory Framework'* and as such serves as an effective, efficient, robust and deadly weapon in the armory of the Entrepreneurs, Tax Practitioners & Taxpayers to combat the hardships and ground-level difficulties and bottlenecks faced by them in their business/professional ventures, amidst the regulatory framework of Income Tax, GST, PF, ESI, Air & Water Pollution Acts etc.

'Learning and improving is a continuous process' and so honest and valuable suggestions and feedback are invited and solicited from the *'worthy readers'*, at my email id mayankmohanka@gmail.com for further improvement.

"व्यये कृते वर्धते नित्यं । विद्या धनं सर्वे धनं प्रधानम् ।।"

Knowledge multiplies manifold by sharing. It is a supreme form of wealth.

About the Author

The Author Sh. Mayank Mohanka, is a seasoned Tax Practitioner, a Fellow Member of the Institute of Chartered Accountants of India and a Bachelor of Commerce, in Honours Degree from Shree Ram College of Commerce (SRCC), Delhi University.

He has a 15+ years of rich and profound experience in the field of Taxation (Direct & Indirect), and Advisory. He makes Representations for a widely diversified cross section of industries including Power Sector, Banking & Finance, Real Estate, Food Processing, Infrastructure, Manufacturing, Education and Information Technology, before Authority for Advance Rulings, ITAT, Education Boards and other appropriate forums.

He has to his credit 35 distinguished, informative, useful and practically oriented published articles in reputed journals, sites and platforms including Taxmann, on wide ranging subjects including Income Tax, GST, PF, ESI, IBC, Corporate Laws, Education Acts & FEMA.

He has also authored a 'Best Seller' Professional Book titled *"Guide to e-Assessment with Real-Time Case Studies & Suggestive e-Submissions"*, with Taxmann Publications, on the New Faceless Income-tax e-Assessments in India.

TAXALOGUE 1

Business Enterprises & Their Struggle through 'Indian Regulatory Framework'!!

Is PM's Vision & FM's Mission of Ensuring 'Ease of Doing Business' Really Fructifying at the Grass Root Level? – A Case Study

The Hon'ble PM Sh. Narendra Modiji's vision and intent of making the philosophy of "Ease of Doing Business" an integral and natural part of the overall business eco-system in our Country and all the tax reforms and rationalisation measures currently being initiated at the behest of the Hon'ble FM Smt. Nirmala Sitharaman, after a series of deliberations and discussions with the representatives of all the stakeholders concerned and the responsive approach of the Finance Ministry is really commendable and deserves appreciation by all quarters.

However, is this virtuous vision, noble intent and sincere efforts at the Top, really percolating downwards and is 'Ease of Doing Business' really happening at the ground and grass root level? This is a million-dollar question which is tried to addressed in this article.

Our Hon'ble PM has scrapped numerous unwanted and outdated Legislative Laws and Acts, in his earnest and sincere endevour towards making the 'Ease of doing business a reality. However, it appears that this is still not enough. Even the bare essential Laws & Regulations concerning the Income Tax, GST, Customs, PF, ESI, Air & Water Pollution Act are enough to act as an effective deterrent in the actual accomplishment of such a noble vision and mission.

The case in point is illustrated here by a real-life case study of a 'Start-up' company, incorporated in India under the 'Make in India' initiative of the Government of India, as a joint venture between a foreign company representing the Foreign National Railways and an Indian company, engaged in the business of manufacturing and supply of locomotive engine parts and components exclusively to the Indian Railways.

The incorporation of this start-up company takes place in a very optimistic business environment with great expectations of operating and functioning in a 'business-friendly environment' with 'ease of doing business' as the guiding philosophy as promised and visioned by the 'top-notch' in the Government.

So, here comes the crucial question i.e. "Is 'Ease of Doing Business' really happening at the ground and grass root level?"

The ensuing journey of this 'start-up' company through the regulatory framework of our country encompassing within its fold the compliances with the respective

Legislative Acts concerning the Environment Clearances (air & water pollution), Income Tax, GST and Provident Fund, to name a few, will help us to reflect upon us the harsh realities of the actual regulatory framework in our country.

(I) Water (Prevention & Control of Pollution) Act, 1974 & Air (Prevention & Control of Pollution) Act, 1981

The start-up company duly obtains the 'Certificate to Establish' (CTE) from the State Pollution Control Board, after fulfilling all the necessary compliances.

After six months, the name of this 'start-up' company gets changed on account of change in the name of the foreign joint venture partner, pursuant to its restructuring. The company duly fulfils all the statutory requirements and ROC formalities for its name change. The company duly intimates the name change to the State Pollution Control Board. The company applies for the 'Certificate to Operate' (CTO) from the State Pollution Control Board after completing and fulfilling all the specified formalities. However, the State Pollution Control Board rejects its application on the ground that at the time of obtaining the CTE, the company's name was different and the company has not taken the prior approval for its name change from the State Pollution Control Board, in the specified format. The company makes its all-out efforts to comply with the specified directions.

In the meanwhile, the company bound by its contractual obligations to manufacture and supply the locomotive engine parts and components viz. pistons, traction motors, alternators and propulsion systems solely and exclusively to the Indian Railways, in a time-bound manner, starts with its manufacturing processes and simultaneously continues with its sincere compliances to obtain the CTO.

However, inspite of its sincere efforts, the company is not given the CTO by the State Pollution Control Board and to the contrary, a 'show cause notice' concerning the proposed closure of its manufacturing set-up u/s 33-A of Water (Prevention & Control of Pollution) Act, 1974 and u/s 31-A of Air (Prevention & Control of Pollution) Act, 1981, within a period of seven days from the receipt of such show cause notice, is being handed over to this start-up company. The company deposits huge amounts as bank guarantees, although under protest, to the State Pollution Control Board, to avoid the proposed closure of its operations.

The entire Regulatory Framework concerning the Air & Water Pollution is aimed at ensuring that the industrial wastes are kept at stipulated benchmarks. In the case of this 'start-up' company, its industrial wastes are kept at minimal levels and even lesser than the stipulated benchmarks. All the requisite processes, procedures and systems are in place in the manufacturing set-up of this company to ensure the reduction of the air and water pollution levels to the minimal levels even much lesser than the stipulated benchmarks. This fact is duly evidenced by the independent and professional test-results of waste, water and air samples, being conducted by an independent Government approved and certified testing agency.

Thus, merely on account of some minor technical and paper-work related irregularities concerning the non-obtaining of the prior approval for its name-change by the State Pollution Control Board in the specified format, the extreme harsh and draconian measure of closure of the industrial operations of the start-up company, especially in the wake of no material evidence, whatsoever, evidencing the creation of any air or water pollution by this company, defeats and makes redundant the very spirit of 'Make in India' initiative of the Government of India and also severely and adversely impacts the lives of thousands of workers and employees of the company who are earning their lively-hoods by way of their employment with this company.

(II) Employees Provident Fund & Miscellaneous Provisions Act, 1952 (EPFMP Act):

For its manufacturing and administrative set-up, the company recruits thousands of skilled and semi-skilled workers and employees and thereby contributes in generation of substantial employment opportunities. The company duly registers itself under the EPFMP Act and duly deposits its PF contribution @12% on basic wages plus DA. In making such contribution towards PF, the company duly and fully adheres to the stipulated condition of fixing the basic wages to atleast 50% the total wages, in view of the Circular No. C-III/110001/4/3(72)14/Circular/Hqrs./6693 dated 6.8.2014 issued by the Regulatory Body EPFO/CPFC. The company does not make any PF contributions on the remaining 50% of total wages constituting different allowances, in view of the official response to one RTI, by the Regulatory Body EPFO – Head Office, Ministry of Labour & Employment, Govt. of India, New Delhi, bearing F.No. C.IV/1(63)10/RTI/948, in October 2010, wherein the EPFO has categorically clarified that the undermentioned allowances are outside the purview of 'basic wages' u/s 2(b) of the Act, and as such don't attract payment of PF contribution, viz.

(a) House Rent Allowance;

(b) Education Allowance;

(c) Conveyance Allowance;

(d) Washing Allowance;

(e) City Allowance;

(f) Leave Travel Allowance;

(g) Night Shift Allowance;

(h) Special Allowance.

However, in the wake of the Hon'ble Supreme Court Judgement in the case of 'RPFC vs. Vivekananda Vidyamandir and others & Surya Roshni Ltd & Ors. vs. The State of Madhya Pradesh EPF RPFC and Ors.' 2019 LLR 339 (SC), holding the allowances as part of basic wages for the purpose of PF contribution, in the cases of the respective parties to this case, the EPFO Field Officers conduct an inspection in the factory premises of this 'start-up' company and hands over a notice u/s 7A of the EPFMP Act, determining the huge liability of the company towards the PF contribution of its employees.

The stand of the Regulatory Body EPFO, Ministry of Labour & Employment, Govt. of India, New Delhi, concerning the non-deduction of PF contribution on allowances, has always been very clear and unambiguous, and as such the establishments, not deducting PF contribution on such allowances, can't be considered as defaulters, with retrospective effect after the above SC Judgement.

Moreover, in the above circular no. C-III/110001/4/3(72)14/Circular/Hqrs./6693 dated 6.8.2014, the regulatory body EPFO/CPFC has itself acknowledged that deduction of PF contribution on more than 50% of the total wages is a sufficient compliance by the establishments so as to do away with the requirement of their inspection by PF authorities. In other words, the Regulatory Body EPFO/CPFC has itself acknowledged that the establishments deducting PF contribution on more than 50% of the total wages of their employees are not indulging in any subterfuge of splitting of wages to reduce the PF liability.

However, unfortunately, a few of the EPFO field officers have started resorting to the outright and blatant misuse of the captioned judgement of the Supreme Court, to put undue pressure on Factories, Shops & Establishments like this 'start-up' company, for PF collections for meeting out their budgetary targets for improving service records, and even for their vested and malafide interests.

Thus, in this particular case, this 'start-up' company was left with no other alternative but to deposit the alleged shortfall in its PF contribution, under protest.

Later on, taking cognizance of its stand that deduction of PF contribution on more than 50% of the total wages is a sufficient compliance by the establishments so as to do away with the requirement of their inspection by PF authorities, the EPFO has issued a Circular No. C-I/I(33)2019/Vivekanand Vidyamandir/717 dated 28.8.2019, directing the Field Officers not to take any adverse action u/s 7A in case of those establishments which have already made PF contributions on atleast 50% of the total wages paid by them to their employees.

However, this 'start-up' company is still battling it out to get its excess PF contribution deposited by it under protest, refunded, from pillar to post.

(III) Income Tax Act, 1961

The 'start-up' company acquires an industrial piece of land out of the share capital funds infused by the joint venture partners after duly complying with all FEMA & SEBI regulatory framework. The State-of-the Art Manufacturing Set-up is established and the latest Plant & Machinery are commissioned and installed by the company.

The fact of "setting-up" of its business by this 'start-up' company is duly evidenced by the undermentioned activities being undertaken by it:

(i) Incorporation under the Companies Act;

(ii) Opening of Current Bank A/cs ;

(iii) Induction of Share Capital Funds for the Business Purposes;

(iv) Acquisition of Land;

(v) Acquisition of Factory Building ;

(vi) Purchase of Plant & Machinery for Manufacturing Set-up;

(vii) Installation and Commissioning of Plant & Machinery;

(viii) Obtainment of Statutory Approvals for Supply of Alternators and Induction Motors to Indian Railways from Research Designs & Standards Organisations (RSDO), Government of India, Ministry of Railways;

(ix) Payment of Engineering & Design Services;

(x) Recruitment of Skilled & Unskilled Staff and their enrolment with EPFO & ESIC Authorities;

(xi) Payment & Disbursal of Staff Salaries and Remunerations.

This 'start-up' company gets a regular assessment notice u/s 143(2) of the Income Tax Act. After a series of deliberations and tedious scrutiny hearings, the assessment boils down to one particular issue concerning the proposed disallowance of expenditure incurred by this start-up company before the commencement of its commercial production.

The concerned Revenue Authority, remains hell bent on treating the entire expenditure incurred by this start-up company during the initial years of its incorporation as pre-operative expenses or expenditure incurred prior to the commencement of business/commercial production, and consider the same as 'capital' in nature.

However, in raising such fundamentally fallacious assertion, the assessing authority somehow overlooks and ignores this well-settled and established principle of Law that in the Income Tax Act, it is only the expenditure which has been incurred prior to the incorporation and prior to the "setting-up of business" by the assessee, which is required to be capitalized. The expenditure incurred after the "setting-up of business" but prior to commencement of business/commercial production is also an allowable expenditure and the cut-off point for considering any expenditure as tax deductible revenue expenditure in the case of a newly incorporated business enterprise or a 'start-up' is "the setting-up of business" and not the "commencement of business".

So, the correct and lawful legal position concerning the allowability of expenditure incurred in case of a newly incorporated business enterprise or a 'start-up' is:

(i) The expenditure incurred prior to the incorporation of an enterprise is to be considered as a pre-incorporation capital expenditure.

(ii) The expenditure incurred prior to the 'setting-up of business' is to be considered as a pre-operative capital expenditure.

(iii) The expenditure incurred after the 'setting-up of business' is to be considered as a tax-deductible revenue expenditure, even if it has been incurred before the commencement of actual business or commencement of commercial production, if it fulfills the mandated conditions u/s 37(1) of the Act.

However, inspite of the above crystal clear and duly evident legal and factual position, the assessing authority remains adamant on making the disallowance of the operating expenditure incurred by this start-up company after its setting up of business, but before the commencement of its commercial production and makes a high-pitched assessment in the hands of this start-up company and the company is forced to deposit atleast 20% of this high pitched demand under protest and is forced to divert its time, energy, efforts and manpower in such unproductive litigations instead of its productive operations.

(IV) CGST & IGST Act:

After one year of gestation period, this start-up company finally starts manufacturing and supplying the locomotive engine parts and components viz. pistons, traction motors, alternators and propulsion systems solely and exclusively to the Indian Railways at very cost effective and competitive prices, resulting in substantial savings in costs and economies of scale for the Indian Railways.

On considerations of the National significance and strategic importance of the Indian Railways, the Legislature has strategically and intentionally provided for an altogether separate and independent Chapter 86 in Section XVII of the Customs Tariff Act dealing exclusively with specific goods and parts and accessories used or supplied exclusively in Railways or Tramway Locomotives, Rolling Stock and parts thereof, and a concessional GST rate of 5% (with no ITC) has been provided on the supply of goods, parts, components and accessories used specifically and exclusively in Indian Railways, falling under that chapter. This legal position has also been given due cognizance by the CBIC in its Circular No. 30/4/2018 dated 25.1.2018.

All the goods and items falling under Chapter 86 in Section XVII of the Customs Tariff Act may be having their respective independent classifications under Chapter 84 or 85 attracting a higher GST rate of 18%/28%, but the very fact of their end usage in Indian Railways, solely and exclusively, entitles them to be classified under Chapter 86 so as to be eligible for a concessional GST rate of 5% (with no ITC).

Any contrary interpretation or conclusion in this regards, will make redundant and defeat the very essence, purpose and Legislative Intent of introducing the separate Chapter 86 in Schedule XVII of the Customs Tariff Act, for goods, parts, components and accessories, used solely and exclusively in Indian Railways, so as to make them eligible for a concessional GST rate of 5% (with no ITC).

However, in the case of this 'start-up' company, contrary to the virtuous intention of the Law-makers in encouraging and promoting the suppliers of locomotive engine parts and components to the Indian Railways, the concerned GST implementing authorities resort to the extreme coercive measure of conducting a search u/s 67 of the GST Act, on the grounds of alleged misclassification of its manufactured goods by this start-up company, under Chapter 86 of Section XVII of the Customs Tariff Act, as against their classification under Chapter 84, of Section XVII of the Customs Tariff Act, attracting a higher GST rate of 18%/28%, as desired and forced by the GST authorities.

Interestingly a plain and simple reading of the provisions as contained in section 67 of the CGST Act, makes it clear and duly evident that the search under this section can be authorised and conducted only if the Competent Authority has reason to believe that:

- any goods liable to confiscation, are secreted in any place; or
- any documents or things which in the opinion of the competent authority will be useful for or relevant to any proceeding under this Act, are secreted in any place.

So, by no stretch of imagination the stated reason of alleged misclassification of the manufactured goods by this start-up company is to be construed or interpreted as an enabling window for formation of reason to believe that any goods liable for confiscation or any relevant documents or things have been secreted by it.

Infact, ironically, it is the due and full disclosure of the stated classification of the imported goods by this company under Chapter 86 of the Customs Tariff Act in its Returns and Audited Books of Accounts, only, on the basis of which the GST authorities have come to know about the same and it is not the case in point that anything has been secreted by this company which needed to be unearthed, by conducting a search.

Thus, unfortunately the sacrosanct window of revoking the provisions of section 67 of the CGST Act, gets being misused and abused by a few of the GST authorities, in this case.

At this juncture, the pathbreaking maiden Union Budget 2019-20 speech of the Hon'ble FM Smt. Nirmala Sitharaman, in the Parliament, needs to be recollected, wherein acknowledging the valuable contribution of taxpayers in the all-round growth of our Nation, She have quoted a wisdom line from Pura Nanooru, a Tamil Sangam Era work by Pisirandaiyaar. The verse ," Yannai pugundha nilam" was sung as an advice to the King Pandian Arivudai Nambi, the English translation of which comes out as under:

"a few mounds of rice from paddy that is harvested from a small piece of land would suffice for an elephant. But what if the elephant itself enters the field and starts eating? What it eats would be far lesser than what it would trample over!"

Unfortunately, in the case of this 'start-up' company, the GST authorities ended up behaving exactly like a mad elephant entering fields and trampling over.

Concluding Remarks:

The 'harsh realities of the actual regulatory environment' as experienced by this 'start-up' company turns out to be diametrically opposite to the idealistic business eco-system as envisaged by our Hon'ble PM & FM, with 'ease of doing business' as its guiding philosophy.

The above stated journey of this 'start-up' company through the compliance gateways of the actual regulatory framework in our Country and the harsh, arbitrary and irrational high handed treatment being coerced upon this 'start-up' company by a few of the so-called 'care-takers'/officials of the Law enforcement agencies and institutions, clearly indicates and evidences that the noble intent and thought process of the Government, the Finance Ministry and the regulatory body CBDT/CBIC in encouraging and rewarding voluntary compliance by taxpayers and ensuring the 'taxpayer friendly regime' is being adversely hampered and distorted to, at the grass root/ground level, by a few over-reaching and over-stretching officials either on account of their dangerous and fatal ignorance of Law or for their vested interests.

Our Hon'ble PM have very dearly coined a term of 'Wealth Creators' for the honest and law-abiding taxpayers like this 'start-up' company, which are contributing their bit towards the growth and prosperity of our Nation and are generating substantial employment opportunities.

However, such unlawful, irrational, adhoc and arbitrary stand and conduct of the few of the over-reaching and over-stretching officials, is acting as a deterrent and a road-block in making the vision of the Hon'ble PM and the mission of the Hon'ble FM, in ensuring and making the philosophy of "Ease of Doing Business" an integral and natural part of the overall business eco-system in our Country, and as such there is an urgent and dire need and necessity for our Hon'ble PM and FM, to issue appropriate directions and instructions to such over-reaching and over-stretching officials, not to act in an irrational and unlawful manner like a trampling elephant entering fields forcefully. It is only then, this noble and guiding philosophy of 'Ease of Doing Business' will become a Reality.

TAXALOGUE 2

Do You Think Tax before Investing?
Personal Investments & Income Tax

"How many millionaires do you know who have become wealthy by investing in savings accounts? I rest my case." — Robert G. Allen

Introduction

1. Given the fact that the return on savings bank deposits is currently so low, it would be foolish to leave one's savings in a savings bank account.

The more conventional personal investment alternatives are shares/securities, real estate properties and funds. Personal Investments decisions are primarily guided by important factors such as rate of return, risk appetite of the investor & time frame of the investments. In addition, one more crucial parameter influencing the personal investment decisions is the Taxation aspect.

In the investment portfolios, it is the *'effective rate of return'* rather than the *'rate of return simpliciter'* which should be the guiding investment criteria. The effective rate of return is the post Income-tax return on investments after taking into account any tax savings.

For instance, consider two investment portfolios, "Portfolio A", consisting of Normal Fixed Deposit (FD) carrying a rate of return of 7% and "Portfolio B", consisting of a Tax-Saver FD u/s. 80C carrying a lower rate of return of 6%, both with time span of 5 years, considering the stipulated lock-in period of 5 years of Tax-Saver FD u/s. 80C. Although the rate of return appears to be higher in Portfolio A, yet, the "effective return" in both the portfolios will be as under:

PARTICULARS	Portfolio A NORMAL FD	Portfolio B TAX SAVER FD u/s. 80C
Investment Amount in INR	1,50,000	1,50,000
Rate of Return	7% p.a. compounded annually	6% p.a. Compounded annually
Returns in Absolute Terms in INR after 5 years Investment*(1+Rate of Return)^5	2,10,383	2,00,734
Income Tax Outflow assuming	63,115*	60,220*

Investor's Tax Bracket of 30%*		
Post Income Tax Returns	1,47,268	1,40,514
Income Tax Savings Impact**	NIL**	45,000**
Total Returns including Tax Saving Impact	1,47,268	1,85,514
* For simplicity sake tax has been calculated at 30% flat rate ignoring surcharge & education cess. ** Investment in tax Saver FD u/s. 80C is eligible for deduction upto Rs. 1,50,000 from the Gross Taxable Income. At the 30% tax bracket, the tax savings impact will come to Rs. 45,000 (30% of Rs. 1,50,000).		

Therefore, the aforesaid example clearly explains that on the basis of rate of return simpliciter, the investor may opt for portfolio A, whereas a further probe into the effective rate of return criteria will definitely alter the investment decision of the investor to opt for portfolio B.

The other popular investments options which are eligible for deduction u/s 80C of the Income Tax Act are investments in Public Provident Fund (PPF), Mutual Funds Equity Linked Savings Scheme (ELSS) & Post Office Savings Schemes. The investors may choose any of these, based on their individual preferences.

Finance Bill, 2018 & its Impact on Personal Investments Decisions

2. Among several other amendments, the most vital amendment, having a direct bearing on personal investment decisions, as brought about by the Finance Bill, 2018, is the withdrawal of existing exemption u/s. 10(38) of the Income Tax Act, in the case of Long Term Capital Gains (LTCG) arising from the transfer of long-term equity shares or units (holding period of 1 or more year), on a recognized stock exchange, and to tax such LTCG, exceeding One Lakh Rupees @ 10%, w.e.f. 1.4.2018.

However, as per the Grandfathering Provisions, The cost of acquisition for the long-term capital asset acquired on or before 31st of January, 2018 will be the actual cost.

However, if the actual cost is less than the fair market value of such an asset as on 31st of January, 2018, the fair market value will be deemed to be the cost of acquisition.

Further, if the full value of consideration on transfer is less than the fair market value, then such full value of consideration or the actual cost, whichever is higher, will be deemed to be the cost of acquisition.

In case of a listed equity share or unit, the fair market value means the highest price of such share or unit quoted on a recognized stock exchange on 31st of January, 2018.

However, if there is no trading on 31st January, 2018, the fair market value will be the highest price quoted on a date immediately preceding 31st of January, 2018, on which it has been traded.

In the case of unlisted unit, the net asset value of such unit on 31st of January, 2018 will be the fair market value.

Taxation of Mutual Funds

3. One of the most popular investment options nowadays, *i.e.*, Mutual Funds, work on the prudent investment policy of *"Don't put all your eggs in one basket"*, *i.e*, Diversification. Mutual Funds can be Equity Oriented Mutual Funds (having 65% or more of their corpus investments in equity or equity linked instruments) or Debt Oriented Mutual Funds (having less than 65% of their corpus investments in equity or equity linked instruments).

MUTUAL FUNDS CAPITAL GAINS TAX RATE: FY 2019-20 (AY. 2020-21)

Type of Mutual Fund Scheme	Short-Term Capital Gains (STCG) Tax Rate	Long-Term Capital Gains (LTCG Tax Rate)
Equity Funds: STCG- Units held for less than 1 year LTCG- Units held for 1 or more than 1 year	15%	10% (without indexation benefit on LTCG exceeding 1 lakhs)
Debt Funds: STCG- Units held for less than 3 years LTCG- Units held for 3 or more than 3 years	As per individuals' tax bracket	20% (with indexation)

Personal Investments & Deemed Taxation u/s. 56(2)(x) of Income-tax Act, 1961

4. The Finance Act, 2017 had inserted a new clause (x) in sub-section (2) of section 56 so as to provide that where any person receives/invests in immovable property:

Without consideration and its stamp duty value exceeds Rs. 50,000, the same would be subject to tax as income from other sources.

For a consideration which is less than the aggregate fair market value of the property determined on the basis of stamp duty value/circle rates, by an amount exceeding fifty thousand rupees, the aggregate fair market value of such property as exceeds such consideration shall be chargeable to tax as 'income from other sources'.

Likewise, where any person invests in/receives any property other than immovable property (shares/securities, etc.) –

> Without consideration, the aggregate fair market value of which exceeds fifty thousand rupees, the whole of the aggregate fair market value of such property shall be chargeable to tax as 'income from other sources'.

> For a consideration which is less than the aggregate fair market value of the property by an amount exceeding fifty thousand rupees, the aggregate fair market value of such property as exceeds such consideration

shall be chargeable to tax as 'income from other sources'.

Fair Market Value (FMV) of Listed/Quotes Shares & Securities is the quoted price in the recognized stock exchange.

FMV of unquoted equity shares = $(A+B+C+D-L) \times PV/PE$, where

A = Book value of all the assets (except those mentioned at B, C and D below) as reduced by income-tax paid (net of refund) and unamortised deferred expenditure

B = Fair market value of jewellery and artistic work based on the valuation report of a registered valuer

C = Fair market value of shares or securities as determined according Rule 11UA of Income-tax Rules.

D = Stamp duty valuation in respect of any immovable property

L = Book value of liabilities, excluding paid-up equity share capital, amount set apart for undeclared dividend, reserves and surplus, provision for tax, provisions for unascertained liabilities and contingent liabilities

PV = Paid-up value of equity shares

PE = Total amount of paid-up equity share capital as shown in the balance sheet.

Dividend Stripping

5. Dividend stripping is an attempt to reduce the tax liability by an investor who invests in securities (*i.e.*, shares, stock or debentures, etc.) and units (Mutual fund units or units of UTI), shortly before the record date and getting a tax free dividend/income, and exiting after the record date at a price lower than the price at which such securities/units were purchased and incurring a short-term capital loss. The strategy behind dividend stripping is a two-way strategy wherein- Investor gets tax free dividend (*i.e.*, exempted u/s. 10(34)/10(35)) Incurs Short term capital loss (*i.e.*, allowed to be set off and carry forward). Record date is the Date fixed by a company or mutual funds for the purpose of entitlement of holders of securities or units to receive dividend or other income.

In order to curb the aforesaid malpractice, provisions of Section 94(7) had been inserted.

6. Conditions to be satisfied to attract the provisions of section 94(7)

Conditions	Securities	Units
Buying or Acquiring	Within a period of 3 months prior to the Record Date	Within a period of 3 months prior

		to the Record Date
Selling or Transferring	Within a period of 3 months after the Record Date	Within a period of 9 months after the Record Date
Dividend or Income during the intervening period	Exempt	Exempt

If all the above mentioned conditions are met, then the short-term capital loss, if any, arising to the investor on purchase and sale of such securities or units, not exceeding the amount of dividend or income received/receivable on such securities or units, shall not be considered while computing the total income chargeable to tax. Even u/s. 94(7) the short-term capital loss arising shall not be allowed to be set-off or carried forward to the extent of dividend or income received.

Bonus Stripping

7. Section 94(8) of the Income-tax Act - 1961, contains the provisions related to the Bonus stripping. Bonus stripping provides that the loss, if any, arising to an

investor on account of purchase and sale of Original units shall be ignored for the purpose of computing his total income chargeable to tax, subject to the following conditions:

7.1 *Conditions to be satisfied to attract the provisions of section 94(8)*

Conditions	Units (Not applicable on Shares)
Buying or Acquiring of Original Units	Within a period of 3 months prior to the Record Date
Allotment of Additional Units	Without any payment on such Record Date
Selling or transferring of Original Units	Within 9 months after the Record date
Holding atleast one Bonus Unit	On the Date of such sale or transfer of original units

If all the above conditions are met, then as per provisions of section 94(8) of the Income- tax Act, the loss arising on account of such sale or transfer of the original units shall be ignored for the purposes of computation of taxable income, and the amount of loss so ignored shall be deemed to be the cost of purchase or acquisition of such bonus units.

Conclusion

8. In Personal Investments Decisions, among other determining factors like nature & type of investments, rate of return, risk profile & appetite of the investor, time frame of investments, etc., the impact of applicability of the relevant provisions of the Direct Taxes on such personal investment decisions is also a significant and crucial consideration, which can't be ignored and possessing the requisite knowledge about the same is a *sine quo non,* for an effective, prudent & lucrative personal investment decision.

Summing up with a well-known investment quote of the renowned author, investment strategist & a philosopher, **Benjamin Franklin,**

"An investment in knowledge pays the best interest."

TAXALOGUE 3

e-Assessments & e-Invoicing
Digital Transformation of Indian Tax
Administration

1. Introduction

Around the world, the momentous advancements in technology, increased digitalisation and the unprecedented flow of information is causing the tax administrations across nations, to re-think and re-examine their conventional and traditional modes of administration to stay effective and non-obsolete and to engage in digital transformation through the introduction of new technologies and analytical tools and to transform into 'digitally mature tax administrations'.

The global tax landscape has been witnessing exponential changes, with tax administrations around the world continuously gearing up to keep pace with the rapid technological advancements to ramp up the effectiveness of their tax administrations.

The use of advanced data analytics, data mining and data processing technologies and automation capabilities, with a keen focus on efficiency, tax-risk management and data-based decision-making, has become a 'mandatory norm' across tax jurisdictions around the world.

According to the Annual Report of 'Forum for Tax Administrations' (FTA) consisting of 53 countries across the world, for the FY 2018-19, 'technology related spending' constituted a significant part of the overall budgets of many revenue bodies around the world, with some of these ranging from 10% to 15% of their total budgets. Various Empirical studies clearly indicate that tax administrations with a high spend on technology witness a correspondingly high rate of compliance. The use of technology has significant potential to improve revenue collection by automation of processes and provision of improved services to taxpayers.

2. International Best Practices concerning Digital Transformation of Tax Administrations:

Tax Administrations worldwide are in the midst of a golden era of innovation and digital transformation. They are continuously upgrading their old tax administration systems or are switching to new ones, in their constant endevours to capture and process the taxpayer-specific relevant information, data and financial transactions on real time basis, using advanced data analytics, data mining and artificial intelligence tools.

The modern-day tax administrations are retrieving and capturing data from business transactions as they occur on real-time basis and are performing advanced analytics and data mining processes, enabling augmentation of revenue collections seamlessly and without any friction with the taxpayers.

International Best Practices concerning Digital Transformation of the Tax Administrations:

(i) Integration with Taxpayers' Natural Accounting Systems;

(ii) Use of Advanced Data Analytics Technology;

(iii) Use of Artificial Intelligence based Algorithms;

(iv) Use of Risk based Taxpayer Profiling;

(v) Digitalisation of Interaction with Taxpayers;

(vi) Automation of Tax Administration Processes;

(vii) Training of Officials for Technical Compatibility.

In addition to these Data Analytics and Processing techniques, Cognitive Computing, Block Chain technology, Artificial Intelligence, and Robotics are prominent examples of technologies that some administrations are already using or exploring. These new technologies offer tax administrations not only further opportunities to improve their efficiency but also enable them to conduct risk-based profiling of the taxpayers and providing mechanisms for 'early warning systems' of potential tax defaulters.

For every enlightened and curious mind, the **Country Specific International Best Practices in Digital Transformation** of Tax Administrations are being discussed as under:

(a) Russia: Integrated Risk Management System (IRM) & Make Tax Digital (MTD)

The Tax Administration Department of Russia, the 'Federal Tax Service' (FTS) has introduced a new system 'Integrated Risk Management System' (IRM) and 'Make Tax Digital' (MTD), which enables it to engage with large business taxpayers to flag tax risks early so that they can be addressed upfront, minimising the risk of future disputes. The IRM system allows the FTS to directly interrogate the accounting information of participating large businesses. It uses a large number of multifactorial risk models built and applied to large data sets through the use of complex algorithms. The embedded data mining functions are able to quickly assess the taxpayer's current operations and predict the probability of future non-compliance. Where such risks are detected, the system automatically generates warnings visible to the taxpayer as well as the tax administration, allowing further enquiries and/or preventative action to be taken at early stages.

(b) Singapore: Leveraging Analytics Design & Digitalisation (LEA:D)

The Tax Administration Department of Singapore, the 'Inland Revenue Authority of Singapore' (IRAS) is aiming to redefine the experiences of both taxpayers and revenue authorities by leveraging analytics, design and digitalisation (LEA:D). The LEA:D initiative is also aligned with Singapore's Smart Nation and Public Sector Transformation initiatives. One of the desired outcomes of LEA:D is to create taxpayer-centred experiences by using an outside-in approach. By first understanding taxpayers' desires and preferences, IRAS seeks to provide convenient and customised digital services to taxpayers. IRAS also collaborates with different players in the tax ecosystem, such as software developers and banks, to increasingly integrate tax into taxpayers' natural systems, providing them with a more seamless tax experience and lowering their compliance costs. To support these digitalisation efforts, IRAS is also modernising its technology platforms and deepening staff competencies in taxpayer-centric service delivery.

(c) Mexico: Servicio de Administración Tributaria (SAT)

The Mexican Tax Administration Department has introduced a new digital platform the 'Servicio de Administración Tributaria' (SAT).

Currently SAT has expanded beyond enabling electronic filing, adding more services online and building databases of information about its taxpayers. The Mexican Tax Administration Department today uses its decade-long digitalization process in two ways: to conduct 360 degree profiling to learn more about taxpayers and also to send 'early warning signals' to the potential tax defaulters, conveying that tax audits (assessments) can be more severe and targeted because of the ready availability of relevant and taxpayer specific data, and thereby prompting voluntary compliance by such potential tax defaulters.

(d) United Kingdom: Advanced Digitised Approval based Assessments

The Tax Administration Department of UK, the 'Her Majesty's Revenue and Customs' (HMRC) has developed such advanced tax administration system that by FY 2020 the taxpayers in UK will not be required to file a tax return.

The tax authorities, based on the information and data concerning the income generation model of the taxpayers, processed by using advanced data analytics techniques, will suo-motto provide the taxpayers with the proposed tax calculations of the reporting period, and taxpayers will have the choice to accept or contest it.

The refunds will be issued promptly instead of allowing them to build up over a tax cycle, and to keep accounts available online and updated in real time, providing a constant and clear picture of the taxpayer's tax position.

(e) Chile: Sales and Acquisitions Electronic Ledger and Pre-filling of VAT returns

In Chile, electronic invoicing is mandatory for B2B transactions (since February, 2018) and about 99% of invoices are issued electronically, providing tax authorities with real-time information on the transactions. The SII has replaced the mandatory VAT ledger with the SAER, which is an electronic register where the tax administration systems register every electronic invoice and tax document issued (Sales Register - output VAT) or received (Acquisitions Register - input VAT) from the taxpayers. In addition, taxpayers are required to upload some information (e.g. invoices issued on paper) in order to reflect accurately their situation and transactions. Based on the data of the SAER, the SII provides the taxpayers with a draft form, which the taxpayers can adjust as necessary. The form contains information such as VAT codes related to invoicing, consumer receipts, credit note and debit note transactions; withholdings for reverse charge invoices; and excess credit from the previous period. Both initiatives represent significant improvements in VAT administration. Regarding the taxpayers, the draft form simplifies and makes the task easier for them, as it comes prefilled with the VAT due to be declared and paid. In addition, as the information is obtained from validated documents, there are fewer errors and inconsistencies in the VAT return process. Regarding the SII, these initiatives resulted in improvements in efficiency and accuracy of VAT inspections and audits due to automatization and better analytical capabilities, and in improvements in risk and fraud detection.

3. Digital Transformation of Indian Tax Administration

Where Does Indian Tax Administration Stands in Comparison to International Best Practices?

"Before embarking upon any new destination, it is wise and prudent to look back at the footprints of the journey made so far...."

India has come a long way in its endeavour to automate tax administration and data processing. The Tax Administration Reform Commission (TARC), under the chairmanship of Dr. Parthasarathi Shome, has recommended extensive use of information and communication technology in administration and governance of taxation system. The Commission emphasised that technology is a critical enabler for the country in its quest to move to modern tax administration. It highlighted areas where technology could play an important role in facilitating and easing tax authorities' interaction with taxpayers and improving compliance. It also elaborates on use of technology in forecasting revenue.

Among the Government's Revenue Departments, the Central Board of Direct Taxes (CBDT) and the Central Board of Indirect Taxes and Customs (CBIC) have always remained pro-active in their approach of making use of modern technology in tax administration.

Both these departments have formulated specific directorates to deal with computerisation-related initiatives and have benefitted significantly in terms of improved compliance, enhanced processing and increased taxpayer satisfaction.

India has been active in leading OECD member countries on the BEPS initiative and has also been an early adopter of automatic exchange of information.

3.1 Key Technology Oriented Initiatives introduced and implemented in the Indian Income Tax Administration System by CBDT:

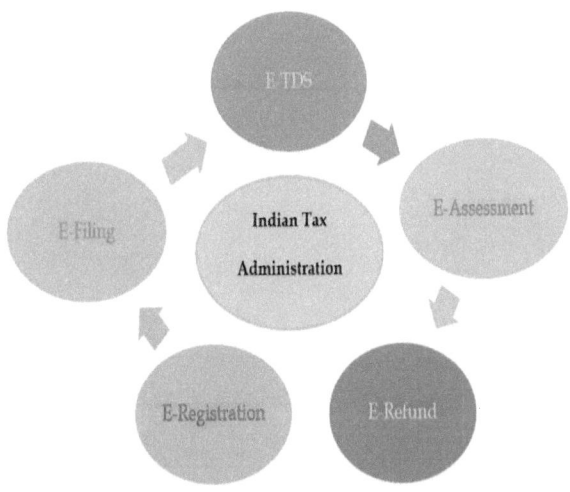

3.1.1 Income Tax Business Application (ITBA)

Very recently the ITD application, which was nearly two decades old, has been substituted and replaced by a new flagship business application, Income Tax Business Application (ITBA), module in the e-Filing portal of the

Income-tax department website with URL **https://www.incometaxindiaefiling.gov.in/home** of the with enhanced capabilities. The new application is intended to comprehensively cover all core processes of the department, including those which were not covered by ITD.

The revolutionary ITBA application facilitates and support, an entire gamut of 'e-services' including:

(a) e-Registration;

(b) e-Filing of ITRs;

(c) e-Proceedings;

(d) e-Payment of Taxes

(e) e-Nivaran

(f) e-Sahyog

(g) e-Submission of Responses to Outstanding Demands

(h) e-Filing of Rectification Application u/s 154 of the Income Tax Act

Gone are the days when the Income-tax Department had to organise camps on the return-filing due date to facilitate filing of returns, and taxpayers had to queue up to obtain stamped acknowledgements. From return filing on hard copies until only a few years ago, e-Filing of Income-tax and TDS returns and their e-Processing by

Central Processing Unit (CPC) and generation of e-Refunds, has now become the order of day for most taxpayers.

3.1.2 360 Degrees Risk Profiling:

The Revenue Authorities, now-a-days, also use technology for risk profiling of taxpayers and transactions to conduct targeted assessments, with specific and pin-pointed enquiries, using the 360 degrees profiling of the taxpayers.

The rapid digital transformation of the Indian Tax Administration system is resulting in a seamless assimilation of different aspects of taxpayer's information such as bank accounts, incomes, expenses and investments through the key field of Permanent Account Number (PAN) and Adhaar.

These data-linkages are expected to increase the tax compliance base, identify defaulters and make enquiries more specific and 'to-the-point'.

Under the Annual Information Return (AIR), considerable information about a taxpayer's activities is being provided to the Tax Authorities. Using such streams of information, the tax administration authorities are having automatic triggers to capture transactions having values disproportionate to a taxpayer's reported income and/or scale of operations. Suspicious transactions could be caught on time. Furthermore, enquiries from Tax Authorities are becoming more specific thereby saving time and effort at both ends and bringing the enquiry to a logical conclusion.

3.1.3 Faceless e-Assessments:

"Artificial Intelligence, Machine Learning, Advanced Data Analytics, Complex Algorithms based Automated Allocation System, Automated Examination Tool, Hash Function, Video Telephony and the list goes on......

*No, any science fiction movie or any space science mission are not being talked about here. Only the 'phraseology' and 'terminology' being used in the recent Official **Gazetted Notification No. SO 3264** issued by the Ministry of Finance on **12.9.2019**, bringing to fore the 'New Scheme of E-assessment 2019', is being referred to here.*

'Welcome to the New Era of 'Faceless', 'Jurisdiction-less', and hopefully 'Corruption-less' E-assessments."

The newest and brightest feather in the *'Digital Indian Tax Administration Cap'* is the introduction of the *'New Scheme of Faceless E-assessment 2019'* encompassing within its fold the use of new technologies like 'machine learning', 'artificial intelligence' and 'advanced algorithm-based data analytical tools', in the conduct of these '**faceless**' and '**jurisdiction-less**' e-assessments.

(a) Faceless Assessments: These assessments are being referred to as **'Faceless'** because these completely eliminate the physical interface between the assessee and the assessing authority and instead involves the complete electronic interface in the conduct of assessments exclusively in electronic mode via the **'e-Proceedings'** utility of the e-Filing portal of Income-tax department's website, and the review and examination of the assessment orders using **'automated examination tool'** involving therein an algorithm for standardised examination of draft assessment orders, by using suitable technological tools, including artificial intelligence and machine learning, with a view to reduce the scope of discretion.

(b) **Jurisdiction-less Assessments:** These assessments are being referred to as **'Jurisdiction-less'** because these are conducted by a Team/Group of Expert IT Officers at multiple-level assessment units viz. National e-Assessment Centre (NeAC), Regional e-Assessment Centre (ReAC), Verification Unit, Technical Unit and Review Unit, and shall not be conducted by an individual jurisdictional Assessing Officer. The cases shall be assigned by NeAC to an assessment unit in any ReAC based on 'automated allocation system' involving therein an algorithm for randomised allocation of cases, by using suitable technological tools, including artificial intelligence and machine learning and as such shall be location agnostic.

This is a welcome and revolutionary transformational move by the Indian Income-tax administration authorities, and is a part of the overall vision & initiative of Digital India.

On 7.10.2019, delivering on the promise made to taxpayers in the budget speech of the Hon'ble Finance Minister, the faceless E-assessment scheme of the Income-tax assessments for the AY 2018-19 and onwards has been launched by the Hon'ble Revenue Secretary, with the inauguration of the National e-Assessment Centre (NeAC) in New Delhi.

In the first phase, out of more than 2.5 lakhs cases selected for scrutiny u/s 143 for the AY 2018-19, the Income-tax department has selected 58,319 cases for scrutiny under the 'New Scheme of E-assessment-2019' more popularly known as the 'Faceless assessments' on pilot basis, and the remaining scrutiny cases are being conducted on the 'e-Proceedings' utility of the e-Filing portal of the Website of the Income-Tax department, as per the existing scrutiny norms.

So, a natural question which comes up in every enlightened mind is as to what is the difference between the existing regular assessments u/s 143(3) being carried out through the e-Proceedings windows and the 'new scheme of e-assessment 2019/faceless e-assessments'.

"To be curious is a good thing and to be able to satisfy someone's curiosity is even better."

Difference between the Assessments through 'e-Proceedings' and the New Scheme of 'E-assessment 2019':

S.No.	Particulars	Existing Assessments through e-Proceedings utility	Faceless E-assessment 2019
1.	Applicability	Assessments u/s 143(3), Assessments u/s 147	Assessment u/s 143(3)
2.	Assessment Year	Till AY 2017-18 and partial cases for AY 2018-19	58,319 cases for AY 2018-19 on Pilot basis
3.	Assessing Authority	Jurisdictional Assessing Officer	National E-assessment Centre (NeAC)
4.	Notice u/s 143(2) Issuing Authority	Jurisdictional Assessing Officer	NeAC, New Delhi
5.	Reply Period of Notice u/s 143(2) & 142(1)	As specified in the Notice u/s 143(2)	Within 15 days from the date of receipt of

			such Notice u/s 143(2)/142(1)
6.	**Assignment of Case**	Jurisdictional Assessing Officer	The NeAC assigns the case to a specific assessment unit in any one Regional E-assessment Centre through an automated allocation system, based on artificial intelligence and machine learning.
7.	**Inquiries during the course of**	Jurisdictional Assessing Officer Issues	The NeAC may issue appropriat

	assessment proceedings	Notices/Questionnaires u/s 142(1) of the Act, for seeking further information, documents or records, from the assessee.	e notice or requisition u/s 142(1) to the assessee for obtaining any further information, documents or evidence as required by the assessment unit in the Regional E-assessment Centre, to which the case has been assigned by the NeAC.

8.	**Provision of Draft Assessment Order**	Only applicable in the Cases of References to Transfer Pricing Officers (TPO) resulting in Variation and Foreign Companies and such Draft Assessment Orders are being passed by the Jurisdictional AOs.	Applicable in all assessments u/s 143(3) of the Act. Draft Assessment Orders are passed by the assessment unit in the Regional E-assessment Centre (ReAC), to which the case has been assigned by the NeAC.
9.	**Action on Draft Assessment Order**	Not Applicable	The NeAC shall examine the draft

| | | | assessment order in accordance with the risk management strategy specified by the Board, including by way of an automated examination tool, whereupon it may decide to: (a) finalise the assessment as per the draft assessment order and serve a |

| | | | copy of such order and notice for initiating penalty proceedings, if any, to the assessee, along with the demand notice, specifying the sum payable by, or refund of any amount due to, the assessee on the basis of such assessment; or |

			(b) provide an opportunity to the assessee, in case a modification is proposed, by serving a notice calling upon him to show cause as to why the assessment should not be completed as per the draft assessment order; or (c) assign the draft assessment

			order to a review unit in any one Regional e-assessment Centre, through an automated allocation system, for conducting review of such order.
10.	**Final Assessment Order**	Passed by the Jurisdictional Assessing Officer after considering the written and verbal submissions of the assessees.	The NeAC sends all the e-replies and submissions of the assessee containing the justification for revision of the draft assessment

			order to the regional assessment unit for revision of the draft assessment order. In the cases, where no objections are filed by the assessees, the NeAC finalises the assessment based on the Draft Order only.

Upon receiving the Revised |

			Draft Assessment Order, the NeAC may:
			(i) in case no modification prejudicial to the interest of the assessee is proposed, finalise the assessment based on such revised draft assessment order; or
			(ii) in case modification

			prejudicial to the interest of the assessee is proposed, an opportunity of personal hearing by way of video telephony only is provided to the assessee, and based on the response of the assessee, the same procedure of revision and finalizatio

			n is to be followed and Final Assessment Order is then passed by the NeAC.
11.	**Mode of Interface between the Assessee and the Assessing Authority**	Electronic Mode via the 'e-Proceedings' functionality in the ITBA Module. However, after serving the Show Cause Notice, an opportunity of Personal Hearing to the assessee involving physical interface between the	Electronic Mode via the 'e-Proceedings' functionality in the ITBA Module. However, after serving the Show Cause Notice, an opportunity of Personal Hearing to the

		assessee and the jurisdictional AO is to be provided.	assessee via video telephony only and without involving any physical interface between the assessee and the NeAC is to be provided.

Live Webcast by ICAI & NeAC, Income-tax Department on the Topic 'Faceless E-Assessments: Issues & Challenges'.

Recently, on 4.12.2019, a live webcast by ICAI & NeAC, Income-tax Department on the topic **'Faceless E-Assessments: Issues & Challenges'**, was being conducted in which the Ld. PCCIT, NeAC, New Delhi, gave his valuable insights and resolved many queries concerning the new scheme of faceless e-assessments.

In the said live webcast on the new scheme of e-Assessments, being conducted jointly by ICAI & NeAC, the author's three queries vide question no. 49 were taken up viz.

(i) First Query: How will revisionary powers of CIT u/s 263/264 be exercised under the new scheme of e-Assessments?

Answer given: Revisionary powers u/s 263/264 shall be exercised after the passing of the final assessment order by NeAC and after transferring of all electronic assessment records to the file of jurisdictional AO, in the same manner as are being exercised at present.

Author's Humble Suggestion: The USP of this new scheme of faceless e-assessments is its 'Team/Group based conduct of e-Assessments by multiple assessment units viz. National e-Assessment Centre (NeAC) and Regional e-Assessment Units (ReAC) including Technical Unit, Verification Unit and Review Unit, in place of the existing individual jurisdictional Assessing Authority (AO).

So, if the final assessment order after being passed by the above multiple assessment units after a comprehensive and diligent review process as underlined in this new scheme, is still being amenable to be revised by an individual jurisdictional CIT, u/s 263, then the finality and conclusivity of such team-based final assessment order, still rests upon the view-points of the individual jurisdictional CIT, which is contrary to the very underlying principle of team-based assessments of this new scheme of faceless e-assessments, and as such suitable amendments should be incorporated in section 263 of the Income-tax Act, in this regards.

(ii) Second Query: Is there any alternative mode of uploading files as attachments along with e-Submissions, other than scanning files?

Answer given: The files may be uploaded in xmls & other modes, however at present these modalities are being worked out.

Author's Humble Suggestion: In the existing 'schema' and 'semantics' of the 'e-Proceedings' functionality, the maximum number of attachments or files which can be attached along with a single 'response' to any notice is 'TEN' (10) and the maximum 'size' of one attachment which can be attached along with a single 'e-response' is '50 MB' of data. Earlier the maximum size of one attachment which can be attached along with a single 'e-response' was 5 MB only. So, in the new scheme of 'E-assessment 2019' the issue of space constraint has been resolved to a great extent. However, the assessees can attach scanned documents only in .pdf, .xls, .xlsx, .csv format.

At times, the process of scanning of files or their conversion into pdf files for the purpose of uploading is very cumbersome and tedious process and involves a lot of time. So, this file conversion becomes an irritant and hinders the smooth and uninterrupted uploading of supporting attachments to be attached `along with the response to any query to a notice.

The requirement of scanning of files or the conversion of files into pdf version to make them up-loadable should be done away with and instead a standard file format like 'XML' in line with the International Best Practice of 'Standard Audit File for Tax' (SAF-T), should be adopted and implemented for uploading files and attachments, by aligning and integrating the 'e-proceedings' functionality of the ITBA module with that of the natural accounting systems of assessees.

(iii) Third Query: In the new scheme of e-Assessments, if say a Delhi based assessee is being assessed by a Mumbai based ReAC based on random allocation system, then Mumbai based ReAC will naturally be guided and influenced by the legal precedents of Mumbai High Court on several crucial scrutiny issues involving interpretation of Law, in conducting the e-assessment, which may differ from the legal precedents of Delhi High Court, on those issues, and applicable on

Delhi based assessee. So, these may result in undue hardships for the Delhi based assessee.

Answer given: It is a complicated issue and suitable measures will be taken to overcome such complexities with the passage of time.

Author's Humble Suggestion: The nodal unit i.e. the NeAC should ensure adopting and following up of the legal precedents of the jurisdictional appellate authorities of the assessees in the conduct of their e-assessments by the assessment units in ReAC.

It is only through continuous, persistent and sincere efforts by the Law-makers and the realistic feedback provided by the assessees as well as the assessing authorities at the ground level, about the desirable improvements in the existing 'e-assessments' functionality, that such revolutionary initiative will get evolved into a more effective, efficient and mature system of Tax Administration over a period of time.

"When solving problems, dig at the roots instead of just hacking at the leaves." -Anthony J. D'Angelo"

For easy and better understanding of the worthy readers, the above stated procedure of 'E-assessment' proceedings as per the new scheme of 'Faceless e-Assessment 2019' is being explained diagrammatically as under:

Diagrammatic Presentation of the New Scheme of E-assessment 2019

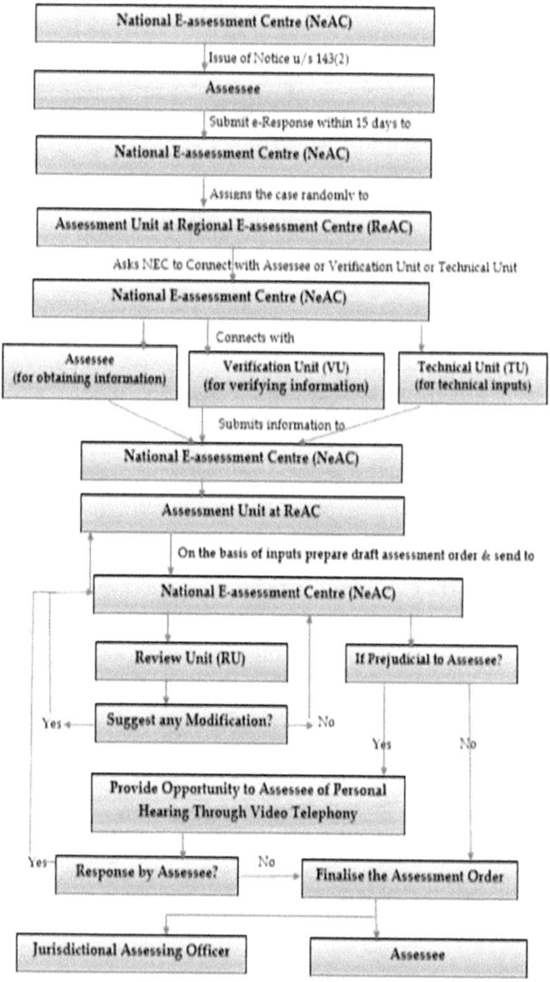

3.1.4 Document Identification Number (DIN):

In order to eliminate the personal discretion of individual income-tax officers in issuing any particular Notice to the assessees, the CBDT vide its Press Release and Circular No. 19/2019 dated 14.8.2019 have mandated that w.e.f. 1.10.2019, all notices, summons, orders and other communications from the Income-tax authorities shall be issued only through a centralised computer system or cell and all such notices and communications shall mandatorily contain a computer generated **'Document Identification Number' (DIN)**, and any communication issued without such 'DIN' shall be considered as nonest in Law.

Procedure for Authenticating all Notices/Requisitions/Letters/Orders received from Income Tax Department using DIN:

Step 1: Visiting the *'e-filing portal'* in Income Tax site:

The assessee has to visit the *'e-filing portal'* in the Income Tax site by visiting the link:

https://www.incometaxindiaefiling.gov.in/home

Step 2: Clicking the hyperlink *'Notice/Order Issued by ITD'* under the tab **'Authenticate'** located at the bottom-left side of the 'e-filing' portal, as shown below:

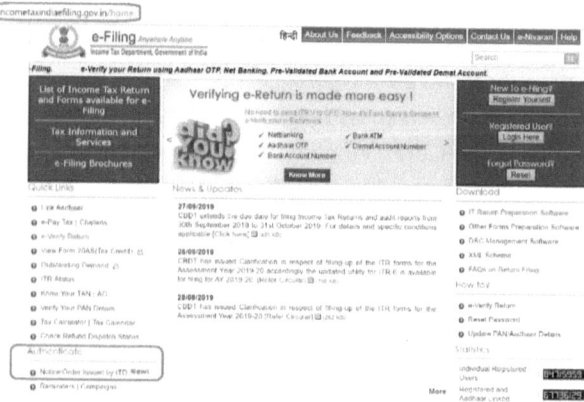

Step 3: In the new window, two search options viz.

    (i)   **Document Number; or**

    (ii)   **PAN, Document Type, Assessment Year & Date of Issue**

will appear.

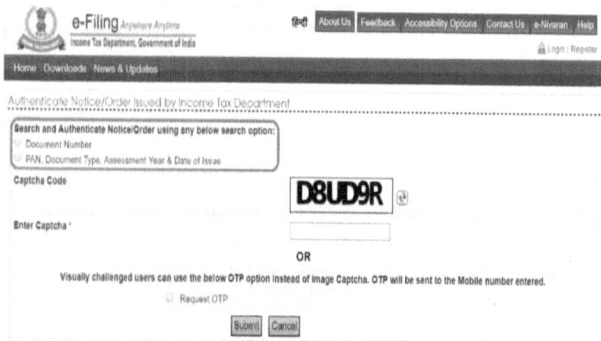

The assessee is required to choose any one of these search options, based upon his convenience and ready availability of the required information needed for the authentication of the Notice/Requisition/Order received from the Income Tax Department.

Step 4(a): If the assessee chooses the search option of **'Document Number'**, then he has to fill in the **'Document Identification Number (DIN)'** mentioned in his Scrutiny Notice/Requisition/Letter/Order, corresponding to the field **'Document Number'** and the **'captcha code'**. After filling in the **'DIN'** and the **'captcha code'**, the assessee is required to click the **'Submit'** radio button.

Step 4(b): If the assessee chooses the search option of **'PAN, Document Type, Assessment Year & Date of Issue'**, then he has to fill in the details of his PAN,

Document Type, Assessment Year & Date of Issue of such Notice or Requisition.

After filling in such details, the assessee is required to fill in the **'captcha code'** and click on the *'Submit'* radio button.

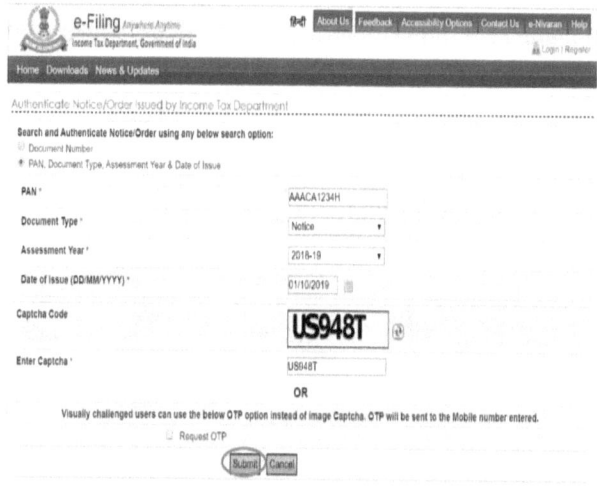

Step 5: Authentication of 'Notice/Requisition/Letter/Order':

The system will authenticate such **Notice/Requisition/Letter/Order** and the assessee can easily check and confirm whether such **Notice/Requisition/Letter/Order** has been issued by authorised and competent Income Tax Authority or not.

Useful Reference: For More Details and Complete Understanding of the nitty-gritties and nuances of the New Scheme of Faceless e-Assessments 2019, the recently published **Book titled "Guide to e-Assessment with Real-time Case Studies & Suggestive e-Submissions"**, authored by the author of this Book, **Sh. Mayank Mohanka, FCA** and published by Taxmann Publications, may be referred, which is a ready referencer and user manual to help and assist the assessees and the assessing authorities in their 'e-Assessment pursuits'. An honest and sincere effort has been made in this Book to explain and demonstrate the practical aspects and nitty-gritties of 'e-Assessments' in a 'step-by-step-manner' through 'real-time practical case studies' encompassing crucial and significant scrutiny issues having immense relevance and practical utility for all the assesses and the assessing authorities. The manner and practical aspects of 'e-filing of Rectification Application' u/s 154 of the Act and 'e-filing of Responses against the outstanding Income Tax demand have also been explained and demonstrated in a 'step-by-step' manner.

3.2 Key Technology Oriented Initiatives introduced and implemented in the Indian Goods & Service Tax Administration System by CBIC:

3.2.1 GSTN Portal:

Following the footprints of CBDT, the CBIC is also making rapid inroads in the digital tax administration initiatives and one such pathbreaking and revolutionary digital initiative is the development and creation of the **'State-of-the-Art GSTN Portal Network'** at the **website gst.gov.in with embedded functionalities of online registration, electronic filing of GST Returns, compliance and invoice level matching of suppliers and recipients for seamless flow of Input Tax Credit (ITC), e-payment of taxes, e-Refunds, e-Way Bill generation.**

3.2.2 e-Invoicing:

Very recently, CBIC have issued five Central Tax notifications on 13.12.2019 i.e. Notification nos. 68/2019, 69/2019, 70/2019, 71/2019, 72/2019 –Central Tax, mandating the preparation and issuance of 'e-Invoices' by a certain specified category of registered persons in GSTN portal by inserting sub-sections (4), (5) and (6) in Rule 48 of CGST Rules 2017, as under:

(i) The functionality of 'e-Invoicing' in the GSTN portal shall be available and effective from 1st January, 2020 on optional basis.

(ii) In case of B2B supplies made by the registered person, whose aggregate turnover in a financial year exceeds one hundred crore rupees, this e-Invoicing mechanism shall be mandatory with effect from 1st April 2020.

(iii) In case of B2C supplies made by a registered person, whose aggregate turnover in a financial year exceeds five hundred crore rupees, to an unregistered person, the e-Invoice shall have QR (Quick Response) code.

(iv) The undermentioned portals shall be used for the purpose of preparation of these e-invoices w.e.f. 1st January 2020:

(a) www.einvoice1.gst.gov.in;
(b) www.einvoice2.gst.gov.in;
(c) www.einvoice3.gst.gov.in;
(d) www.einvoice4.gst.gov.in;
(e) www.einvoice5.gst.gov.in;
(f) www.einvoice6.gst.gov.in;
(g) www.einvoice7.gst.gov.in;
(h) www.einvoice8.gst.gov.in;
(i) www.einvoice9.gst.gov.in;
(j) www.einvoice10.gst.gov.in.

3.2.3 Document Identification Number (DIN):

In keeping with the Government's objectives of transparency and accountability in indirect tax administration through widespread use of information technology, following the footsteps of CBDT, the CBIC vide its Notification No. 122/41/2019-GST has mandated a system for electronic (digital) generation of a **Document Identification Number (DIN)** for all communications sent by its offices to taxpayers and other concerned persons.

The CBIC in exercise of its power under section 168(1) of the CGST Act, 2017/ Section 37B of the Central Excise Act, 1944 has directed that no search authorization, summons, arrest memo, inspection notices and letters issued in the course of any enquiry shall be issued by any officer under the Board to a taxpayer or any other person, on or after the 8th day of November, 2019 without a computer-generated Document Identification Number (DIN) being duly quoted prominently in the body of such communication. The digital platform for generation of DIN is hosted on the Directorate of Data Management (DDM)'s online portal "**cbicddm.gov.in**"

The Board has also directed that any specified communication which does not bear the electronically generated DIN and is not covered by the specified exceptions, shall be treated as invalid and shall be deemed to have never been issued.

This measure would create a digital directory for maintaining a proper audit trail of such communication. Importantly, it would provide the recipients of such communication a digital facility to ascertain their genuineness.

4. Concluding Remarks:

"The only thing which is constant is the change!!

In order to make these path-breaking, radical and revolutionary initiatives of the CBDT and CBIC aimed at ensuring digital transformation of the Indian Tax Administration System, effective and taxpayer friendly, it is essential and crucial to ensure the commensurate and supporting IT infrastructure to enable seamless and smooth data transfer, incorporating standardization in the conduct of assessments by assessing authorities by implementing Standard Operating Procedures (SOPs) to do away with the subjective-ness and arbitrariness in making additions and disallowances in 'e-assessments' and fixing proper and effective accountability in cases of high pitched assessments.

All the stakeholders involved i.e. the taxpayers, the tax professionals, the assessing authorities, the regulatory bodies CBDT & CBIC, the Finance Ministry and the Government should embrace these radical, revolutionary and path-breaking digital reforms in good and positive spirits and should work collectively and cohesively to make these initiative a grand success.

"Innovation means replacing the best practices of today with those of tomorrow." — Paul Sloane

TAXALOGUE 4

Income & Expenditure pertaining to Pre-Commencement Business Period: Revenue or Capital?

"To be curious is a good thing and to work towards satisfying ones' curiosity is even better."

Introduction:

The critical question concerning the nature and taxability of 'income' and 'expenditure' pertaining to the 'pre-commencement business/commercial production' period, in newly incorporated business enterprises and 'start-ups' has always remained a confusing and litigative issue with Revenue Authorities considering the expenses as capital in nature and income as revenue in nature and the assessees wishing to treat the same in exactly the opposite manner.

In this 'article' an honest and sincere attempt has been made to eliminate the confusion and uncertainty regarding this conundrum and to facilitate a clear and better understanding of the entire issue by analysing all significant and prominent legal precedents in this regard.

(A) Nature & Tax Implications of 'Expenditure' pertaining to pre-commencement business/commercial production' period:

The Revenue Authorities, as per their natural tendency of augmenting revenue collections, tend to treat the entire expenditure incurred by the business enterprises and 'start-ups' during the initial years of their incorporation as pre-operative expenses or expenditure incurred prior to the commencement of business/commercial production, and consider the same as 'capital' in nature to be debited to the 'Capital Work In Progress" a/c, till the time period of commencement of actual business/commercial production and to be proportionately amortised in subsequent years.

No doubt, it is a well settled and established principle of Law that any expenditure incurred prior to the incorporation of a business enterprise is a capital expenditure. It is also not doubtful that for any expenditure to become eligible to be claimed as tax deductible revenue expenditure u/s 37(1) of the Income Tax Act, it is a mandatory pre-requisite that such expenditure should have been incurred solely and exclusively for business purpose and it should be revenue in nature.

So, the natural and simplistic belief of the Assessing Authorities concerning the tax treatment of 'expenditure' pertaining to the pre-commencement business period, centers around the philosophy that *"when the business has not commenced, how can there be any question of claiming any tax-deductible business expenditure by the assessee?"*

Now, a natural question crops up in every enlightened mind as to what constitutes "commencement of business"? In simple words, when can a business be said to be commenced?

Again, the Revenue Authorities have very simplistic answer to this otherwise complicated question and that is in case of manufacturing concerns the business is deemed to be commenced when the commercial production commences and in trading concerns the execution of first trading order embarks the commencement of business.

However, this simplistic approach of Revenue Authorities results in very complicated situations for the business enterprises and 'start-ups' wherein the entire expenditure incurred by these enterprises during their initial years of incorporation is being denied to be claimed as lawful business expenditure, on the ground that actual business has not started or commercial production has not commenced.

Is this simplistic approach of the Revenue Authorities, a correct approach and in conformity with the established principles of Law? This is indeed a million-dollar question and this 'write-up' tries to address this issue.

Interestingly, in the entire framework of the existing Direct Taxation Law, no-where it is stipulated or mandated that for claiming any lawful business expenditure, the commencement of business or the commencement of commercial production is a mandatory pre-requisite or a sine-quo-non. Infact the terminology "commencement of business" itself does not find any place in any of the sections of the Income Tax Act, and as such, the widely prevailing notion and belief of 'non-allowability of expenditure incurred prior to the commencement of business', has infact no statutory backing of the Governing Act i.e. The Income Tax Act, 1961.

So, then what is the correct and actual position of Law in this regard? Again, the Governing Law only comes to rescue to address this complicated question.

"When in confusion and dilemma en-route any journey, begin from the beginning again."

So, in our quest to find a plausible answer to the above question, it is desirable and worthwhile to begin from the very beginning of the sections as contained in the Income Tax Act- the trigger point of the incidence of tax for any business enterprise, *"its first previous year".*

Proviso to section 3 of the Income Tax Act defines the term **"previous year"** in the context of any business enterprise or 'Start-Up' being newly incorporated and set-up.

For ready reference the text of section 3 and its proviso is being reproduced as under:

"Previous year" defined.

3. For the purposes of this Act, "previous year" means the financial year immediately preceding the assessment year:

Provided that, in the case of a business or profession newly set up, or a source of income newly coming into existence, in the said financial year, the previous year shall be the period beginning with the date of setting up of the business or profession or, as the case may be, the date on which the source of income newly comes into existence and ending with the said financial year."

So, a plain reading of the above provision clearly shows that for a new business or 'start-up', the 'previous year' is the period beginning with the date of 'setting up of the business'.

As explained by the Hon'ble Bombay High Court in the case of *"M/s. Western India Vegetable Products Limited"*:

"once it is known what the business of an assessee is, the important question that has got to be considered is from which date are the expenses of this business to be considered permissible deductions and for that purpose the section that we have got to look to is Section 2(31) and that section defines the 'previous year' and for the purpose of a business the previous year begins from the date of setting up of the business. Therefore, it is only after the business is set up that the previous year of that business commences and in that previous year the expenses incurred in the business can be claimed as permissible deductions. Any expenses incurred prior to setting up of a business would obviously not be permissible deductions because those expenses would be incurred at a point of time when the previous year of the business would not have commenced."

Thus, from above, it is duly evident and amply clear that **the cut-off point for considering any expenditure as tax deductible revenue expenditure in the case of a newly incorporated business enterprise or a 'start-up' is "the** setting-up of business" and not the "commencement of business", as is being widely believed, or rather mis-believed.

The expression *"setting-up of business"* is **not synonymous** with the expression *"commencement of business/commercial production"*.

The business is said to be "set-up" when it is "ready to commence business" and actual commencement is not relevant for "setting up of the business". The setting up of business is usually a stage anterior to commencement of business and there can be a time interval between the two events.

So, the correct and lawful legal position concerning the allowability of expenditure in case of a newly incorporated business enterprise or a 'start-up' is:

(i) The expenditure incurred prior to the incorporation of an enterprise is to be considered as a pre-incorporation capital expenditure.

(ii) The expenditure incurred prior to the 'setting-up of business' is to be considered as a pre-operative capital expenditure.

(iii) The expenditure incurred after the 'setting-up of business' is to be considered as a tax-deductible revenue expenditure, even if it has been incurred before the commencement of actual business or commencement of

commercial production, if it fulfills the
mandated conditions u/s 37(1) of the Act.

So, now after having clarity over the issue of cut-off point for the allowability of any business expenditure in the case of a newly incorporated business enterprise or a 'start-up' to be "the setting-up of its business" and not the "commencement of its business", the next big question that comes to any curious mind is as to:

What constitutes "setting-up of business"?

The Hon'ble Delhi High Court in the case of *"Care four WC & C India (P.) Ltd. v. DCIT" [2015] 53 taxmann.com 289 (Delhi)*, after referring to its numerous previous judgements, have very comprehensively and beautifully analysed and explained the concept of "setting up of business" and have observed that to 'set-up a business', the following activities become relevant:

"Preparation of a business plan; establishment of a business premises; research into the likely markets or profitability of the business; acquiring assets for use in the business; obtaining registration as an entity and under the local laws, opening of bank account; recruitment of personnels, obtaining licenses, obtaining orders etc."

Over a period of time, different High Courts and even the Hon'ble Supreme Court have adjudicated the issue of allowability or otherwise of expenditure incurred by a newly incorporated business enterprise or a 'start-up' and in the process of such adjudication have laid down some well settled and established testimonials to the concept of 'setting-up of business' and have categorically held that any operating business expenditure incurred by an enterprise after the 'setting-up of its business' is fully allowable tax-deductible revenue expenditure, even if it has been incurred prior to the commencement of business or commercial production.

Some of the prominent and significant judgements in this regard and their citations are enumerated below, for the sake of ready reference:

(i) CIT w Sarabhai Management Corporation Ltd (1991) 192 ITR 151 (SC);

(ii) CIT vs. Hughes Escorts Communications Pvt Ltd" (311 ITR 253) (Delhi High Court);

(iii) CIT vs Whirlpool of India Ltd. 318 ITR 347 (Delhi High Court);

(iv) CIT vs L.G. Electronics (I) Ltd. 282ITR 545 (Delhi High Court);

(v) CIT vs. ESPN Software India (P) Ltd. 301 ITR 368 (Delhi High Court);

(vi) CIT vs. Aspentech India (F) Ltd." [2010] 187 Taxman 25 (Delhi High Court);

(vii) CIT vs. E. Funds International India, [2007] 162 Taxman 1 (Delhi High Court);

(viii) CIT Vs. Dhoomketu Builders & Development Pvt. Ltd., 216 Taxman 76;

(ix) CIT Vs. Samsung India Electronics Limited, 356 ITR 354;

(x) CIT Vs. Franco Tosi Ingegnaria, 241 ITR 268;

- *(xi)* *CIT Vs. Western India Seafood (P) Ltd., 199 ITR 777;*
- *(xii)* *CIT Vs. Saurashtra Cement & Chemicals Industries Ltd., 91 ITR 170;*
- *(xiii)* *DCIT vs. Jatra Ruchi Cosmetics ITA No 5877/Del/2015 dated 20.2.2019 (Delhi ITAT);*

Based on a thorough analysis of the above judgements, a ready referral guide or pointer to the activities constituting the 'setting-up of business' of an enterprise is provided below for the sake of brevity and clear understanding.

Activities evidencing "Setting-up of Business" in a Business Enterprise/Start-Up:

- (i) Incorporation & Registration under the various Governing Acts like, the Companies Act; the Factories, Shops & Establishment Act; the CGST & IGST Act etc.
- (ii) Opening of Bank A/c ;
- (iii) Induction of Share Capital Funds for the Business Purposes;
- (iv) Acquisition/Leasing of Land;
- (v) Acquisition/Construction/Renting of Office Building and Premises;
- (vi) Acquiring Assets for use in the business;
- (vii) Installation & Commissioning of Plant & Machinery;
- (viii) Obtainment of Statutory Approvals & Licenses for business purpose;

- (ix) Obtainment of Electricity and Water Connection;
- (x) Recruitment of Skilled & Unskilled Staff and their enrollment with EPFO & ESIC Authorities;
- (xi) Payment & Disbursal of Staff Salaries and Remunerations.
- (xii) Preparation of a Business Plan;
- (xiii) Research into the likely Markets or Profitability of the business;
- (xiv) Participating in Tenders for business procurement;
- (xv) Obtaining Business Orders;

Thus, the newly incorporated business enterprises and start-ups having undertaken the above mentioned one or more gamut of activities ought to be considered to have achieved the status of 'setting-up of business', as per the criteria and tests laid out by the Hon'ble High Courts, and the operating expenditure incurred by such enterprises after the 'setting up of their business' ought to be considered as tax-deductible revenue expenditure, even if it has been incurred before the commencement of business or commercial production, if it meets the stipulated conditions as envisaged u/s 37(1) of the Income Tax Act viz.

- (i) The expenditure should have been incurred solely and exclusively for the business operations of the assessee.
- (ii) The expenditure should be of revenue in nature.

(iii) The expenditure should not be of personal nature.
(iv) The expenditure should not be expressly disallowed under any other section of the Income Tax Act.

(B) Nature & Tax Implications of 'Income' pertaining to 'pre-commencement business/commercial production' period:

It is not uncommon for the newly incorporated business enterprises and 'start-ups' to temporarily park their share capital contributions and/or borrowed funds in Bank Fixed Deposits or other similar investment avenues to earn interest or other similar income prior to the commencement of business/ commercial production, in order to augment and optimize their project resources or to minimize their project costs.

As the Revenue Authorities tend to consider the 'expenditure' incurred by business enterprises or 'start-ups' during the pre-commencement business period as capital in nature, one would be inclined to believe that the Authorities would adopt the consistency in treating such income earned during this period to be also of capital in nature.

However, the Revenue Authorities are not so consistent after all….

Contrary to their consideration of expenditure pertaining to the pre-commencement of business period, as a capital expenditure, the Revenue Authorities, usually treat the interest and any other similar income earned by the enterprises during this period as revenue in nature, and in doing so, the Authorities most often quote the decision of the Hon'ble Supreme Court in the case of *"Tuticorin Alkali Chemicals and Fertilisers Ltd vs. CIT*" reported in 227 ITR 172.

A blanket and blind application of the said judgement of the Hon'ble Supreme Court, without going into its nitty-gritties and details and without even understanding the actual ratio emerging out of the said judgement, is being resorted to, in considering each and every income pertaining to the pre-commencement business period, as revenue in nature.

In the said case of 'Tuticorin Alkali Chemicals' [1997] 227 ITR 172, it was found by the authorities that the borrowed funds, being surplus and idle, were utilized by the assessee in investing in fixed deposits to earn interest income and, therefore, the Hon'ble Supreme Court have held that the interest earned on surplus borrowed funds would have to be treated as "Income from other sources".

However, in numerous subsequent judgements of the Hon'ble Supreme Court and the Hon'ble High Courts, in the cases of:

(i) "Bokaro Steel Ltd. [1999] 236 ITR 315 (SC)"; (i)
(ii) CIT vs Karnal Co-operative Sugar Mills Ltd 243 ITR 2 (SC);
(iii)CIT vs Karnataka Power Corporation 247 ITR 268 (SC);
(iv) Bongaigaon Refinery And Petrochemicals Ltd. v. Commissioner of Income-Tax, [2001] 251 ITR 329 (SC);

(v) Indian Oil Panipat Power Consortium Ltd vs. ITO 315 ITR 255 (Delhi High Court);
(vi) CIT vs Jaypee Dsc Ventures Ltd in ITA No. 357/2010 (Delhi High Court);
(vii) PCIT vs Facor Power Ltd (2016) 66 Taxmann.com (Delhi High Court);
It has been categorically held that if the income is earned whether by way of interest or in any other manner on the funds which are otherwise inextricably linked to setting up of the plant for business purpose, such income is required to be capitalised to be set off against preoperative expenses.

At this juncture, it would be desirable and worthwhile to bring the worthy readers' kind attention to the categorical observations and findings of the Hon'ble Delhi High Court in the case of **"Indian Oil Panipat Power Consortium Ltd vs. ITO"** 315 ITR 255" wherein the Hon'ble Delhi High Court have held as under:

"5. In our opinion the Tribunal has misconstrued the ratio of the judgment of the Supreme Court in the case of Tuticorin Alkali Chemicals (supra) and that of Bokaro Steel Ltd. (supra). The test which permeates through the judgment of the Supreme Court in Tuticorin Alkali Chemicals (supra) is that if funds have been borrowed for setting up of a plant and if the funds are surplus and then by virtue of that circumstance they are invested in fixed deposits the income earned in the form of interest will be taxable under the head "income from other sources. On the other hand the ratio of the Supreme Court judgment in Bokaro Steel Ltd. (supra) to our mind is that if income is earned, whether by way of interest or in any other

manner on funds which are otherwise inextricably linked to the setting up of the plant, such income is required to be capitalized to be set off against pre-operative expenses.

5.2. It is clear upon a perusal of the facts as found by the authorities below that the funds in the form of share capital were infused for a specific purpose of acquiring land and the development of infrastructure. Therefore, the interest earned on funds primarily brought for infusion in the business could not have been classified as income from other sources. Since the income was earned in a period prior to commencement of business it was in the nature of capital receipt and hence was required to be set off against pre-operative expenses.

In the case of Tuticorin Alkali Chemicals [1997] 227 ITR 172 it was found by the authorities that the funds available with the assessee in that case were "surplus" and, therefore, the Supreme Court held that the interest earned on surplus funds would have to be treated as "Income from other sources". On the other hand in Bokaro Steel Ltd. [1999] 236 ITR 315 (SC) where the assessee had earned interest on advance paid to contractors during pre- commencement period was found to be "inextricably linked" to the setting up of the plant of the assessee and hence was held to be a capital receipt which was permitted to be set off against pre-operative expenses."

Thus, the ratio of the judgment of the Hon'ble Supreme Court in the case of 'Tuticorin Alkali Chemicals' (supra) and that of 'Bokaro Steel Ltd.' (supra), is often misconstrued by the assessing authorities and even by the tax professionals.

The real test which permeates through the judgment of the Hon'ble Supreme Court in 'Tuticorin Alkali Chemicals' (supra) is that if funds have been borrowed for setting up of a plant and if the funds are surplus and then by virtue of that circumstance they are invested in fixed deposits the income earned in the form of interest will be taxable under the head "income from other sources.

On the other hand, the ratio of the Hon'ble Supreme Court judgment in 'Bokaro Steel Ltd.' (supra), is that if income is earned, whether by way of interest or in any other manner on funds which are otherwise inextricably linked to the setting up of the plant, such income is required to be capitalized to be set off against pre-operative expenses.

Concluding Remarks:

Even at the cost of repetition, in view of enabling clear understanding and ready reference, it is worthwhile and desirable to summarise the above discussed propositions concerning the nature and tax implications of 'Expenditure' and 'Income' pertaining to the pre-commencement business/commercial production period, in the case of newly incorporated business enterprises and 'start-ups', as under:

(A) Pre-Commencement Business Expenditure:
 (i) **The expenditure incurred prior to the incorporation of an enterprise is to be considered as a pre-incorporation capital expenditure.**

(ii) The expenditure incurred prior to the 'setting-up of business' is to be considered as a pre-operative capital expenditure.

(iii) The expenditure incurred after the 'setting-up of business' is to be considered as a tax-deductible revenue expenditure, even if it has been incurred before the commencement of actual business or commencement of commercial production, if it fulfills the mandated conditions u/s 37(1) of the Act.

(B) Pre-Commencement Interest & Other Income:

(i) Interest and other similar income earned by way of investment of 'surplus' and 'idle' share capital or borrowed funds in bank fixed deposits or other similar investment avenues, with a specific view of earning such income, is revenue in nature and is taxable under the head 'income from other sources'.

(ii) Interest and other similar income earned by way of temporary investment of share capital or borrowed funds, which are otherwise inextricably linked to the setting up of the business plant or infrastructure or such similar business operations, with a specific view to make efficient use of the project capital and to thereby reduce the cost of the project, is capital in nature and is required to be set off against pre-operative expenses.

It is a cardinal principal and trite law that the Assessing Authority is a Quasi-Judicial Authority and as such it is duty bound to assess and collect only legitimate and due taxes from the assessee as per Article 265 of the Constitution of India.

Article 265 of the Constitution of India lays down that no tax shall be levied except by authority of law. Hence only legitimate tax can be recovered and even an omission by an assessee does not give authority to the tax collector to recover more than what is due from him under the law.

It is also worthwhile to mention here that CBDT has itself acknowledged the above proposition as stipulated in Article 265 of the Constitution of India, by way of a Circular No: 14 (XL-35) dated April 11, 1955, wherein it has been stated that:

"Officers of the Department must not take advantage of ignorance of an assessee as to his rights. It is one of their duties to assist a taxpayer in every reasonable way, particularly in the matter of claiming and securing reliefs and in this regard the Officers should take the initiative in guiding a taxpayer where proceedings or other particulars before them indicate that some refund or relief is due to him. This attitude would, in the long run, benefit the Department for it would inspire confidence in him that he may be sure of getting a square deal from the Department. Although, therefore, the responsibility for claiming refunds and reliefs rests with assessee on whom it is imposed by law, officers should:

(a) Draw their attention to any refunds or reliefs to which they appear to be clearly entitled but which they have omitted to claim for some reason or other;

(b) Freely advise them when approached by them as to their rights and liabilities and as to the procedure to be adopted for claiming refunds and reliefs."

Therefore, it is desirable on the part of the Assessing Authorities who hold such a responsible and respectable position of a Quasi-Judicial Authority in the Legislature, to take due cognizance and recognition of the above stated well settled and established principles of Law concerning the nature and taxability of 'income' and 'expenditure' pertaining to the pre-commencement business/commercial production period and to conduct assessments of the newly incorporated business enterprises and the 'start-ups' involving the issues concerning such 'income' and 'expenditure', by adhering to the principles of natural justice, equity and fair-play, in order to ensure and facilitate the much needed boost and fillip to the "Start-Ups" segment, in real and effective manner.

TAXALOGUE 5

Colourable Devices vs. GAAR

Colours represent Vibrancy in Holi Festival...But in Income Tax Act, what do they signify?

The Festival of Holi is unthinkable without colours. The use of colours by way of different devices like pichkaris, balloons, pumps, and even buckets, constitutes an essential ingredient of a vibrant, joyful and blissful Holi. However, in Income Tax Act, the expression, *"colourable device"*, is being looked at, in an altogether different manner.

In its landmark judgment, in the case of **"McDowell and Company Ltd vs. Commercial Tax Officer, 154 ITR 148**, the Hon'ble Supreme Court, has held that,

"The Tax Planning may be legitimate provided it is within the framework of law. Colourable Devices cannot be part of tax planning..."

The thin dividing line between "legitimate tax planning" and "illegitimate tax evasion", started getting blurred, after the misinterpretation of the said judgement by the Revenue Authorities, until the Hon'ble Supreme Court, in its another landmark judgement, in the case of **"Union of India vs. Azadi Bachao Andolan and Anr 263 ITR 706"**, again re-inforced and re-instated the legal sanctity of the said divide between "legitimate tax planning" and "illegitimate tax evasion". The Hon'ble Apex Court, had observed,

*"We may in this connection usefully refer to the judgement of the Madras High Court in M.V. Vallipappan and others v. ITO, which has rightly concluded that **the decision in McDowell cannot be read as laying down that every attempt at tax planning is illegitimate and must be ignored, or that every transaction or arrangement which is perfectly permissible under law, which has the effect of reducing the tax burden of the assessee, must be looked upon with disfavour**…..*

*We may also refer to the judgement of Gujrat High Court in Banyan and Berry v. CIT, where referring to McDowell, the court observed: **"The court nowhere said that every action or inaction on the part of the taxpayer which results in reduction of tax liability to which he may be subjected in future, is to be viewed with suspicion and be treated as a device for avoidance of tax irrespective of legitimacy or genuineness of the act;** an interference which unfortunately, in our opinion, the Tribunal, apparently appears to have drawn from the enunciation made in McDowell case (1985) 154 ITR 148 (SC). The ratio of any decision has to be understood in the context it has been made. **The facts and circumstances which lead to McDowell's decision leave us in no doubt that the principle enunciated in the above case has not affected the freedom of the citizen to act in a manner according to his requirements, his wishes, in the manner of doing any trade, activity or planning his affairs, with circumspection, within the framework of law, unless the same fall in the category of colourable device which may*** *properly be called a device or a dubious method or a subterfuge clothed with apparent dignity."*

Then again in its historic judgement in the case of **"Vodafone International Holdings B.V. vs. Union of India & Anr."**, the Hon'ble Supreme Court had observed with subtle clarity as under,

"The department's argument that there is a conflict between Azadi Bachao Andolan 263 ITR 706 (SC) & McDowell 154 ITR 148 (SC) and that Azadi Bachao is not good law is not acceptable. While tax evasion through the use of colourable devices and by resorting to dubious methods and subterfuges is not permissible, it cannot be said that all tax planning is impermissible."

With these landmark judgments, a well settled legal position regarding the re-enforcement of the legal sanctity of the "legitimate tax planning" as against the "use of colourable devices for illegitimate tax evasion", was emerging…..

With the Advent of GAAR, Is the Thin Dividing Line between "Legitimate Tax Planning" & "Illegitimate Tax Evasion" Getting Further Blurred???

A new Chapter X-A, containing sections 95 to 102, has been incorporated, in the Income Tax Act. After its deferment in a couple of Finance Acts, finally, it has been made applicable w.e.f. AY 2018-19.

In simple words, under the GAAR regime, any arrangement, the main purpose of which is to obtain a

tax benefit and which lacks commercial substance, would be considered as an impermissible avoidance arrangement.

For the sake of ready reference, the text of relevant sections as contained in Chapter X-A, is being reproduced as under:

Applicability of General Anti-Avoidance Rule.

95.(1) *Notwithstanding anything contained in the Act, an arrangement entered into by an assessee may be declared to be an impermissible avoidance arrangement and the consequence in relation to tax arising therefrom may be determined subject to the provisions of this Chapter.*

[(2) This Chapter shall apply in respect of any assessment year beginning on or after the 1st day of April, 2018.]

Explanation. – For the removal of doubts, it is hereby declared that the provisions of this Chapter may be applied to any step in, or a part of, the arrangement as they are applicable to the arrangement.

Impermissible avoidance arrangement.

96.(1)*An impermissible avoidance arrangement means an arrangement, the main purpose of which is to obtain a tax benefit, and it –*
- *(a) creates rights, or obligations, which are not ordinarily created between persons dealing at arm's length;*
- *(b) results, directly or indirectly, in the misuse, or abuse, of the provisions of this Act;*
- © *lacks commercial substance or is deemed to lack commercial substance under section 97, in whole or in part; or*

(d) is entered into, or carried out, by means, or in a manner, which are not ordinarily employed for bona fide purposes.

(2) An arrangement shall be presumed, unless it is proved to the contrary by the assessee, to have been entered into, or carried out, for the main purpose of obtaining a tax benefit, if the main purpose of a step in, or a part of, the arrangement is to obtain a tax benefit, notwithstanding the fact that the main purpose of the whole arrangement is not to obtain a tax benefit

Arrangement to lack commercial substance.

97. (1) An arrangement shall be deemed to lack commercial substance, if —
- *(a) the substance or effect of the arrangement as a whole, is inconsistent with, or differs significantly from, the form of its individual steps or a part; or*
- *(b) it involves or includes —*
  - *(i) round trip financing;*
  - *(ii) an accommodating party;*
  - *(iii) elements that have effect of offsetting or cancelling each other; or*
  - *(iv) a transaction which is conducted through one or more persons and disguises the value, location, source, ownership or control of funds which is the subject matter of such transaction; or*
- *(c) it involves the location of an asset or of a transaction or of the place of residence of any party which is without any substantial commercial purpose other than obtaining a tax benefit (but for the provisions of this Chapter) for a party; or*
- *(d) it does not have a significant effect upon the business risks or net cash flows of any party to the arrangement apart*

from any effect attributable to the tax benefit that would be obtained (but for the provisions of this Chapter).

(2) *For the purposes of sub-section (1), round trip financing includes any arrangement in which, through a series of transactions –*
   (a) *funds are transferred among the parties to the arrangement; and*
   (b) *such transactions do not have any substantial commercial purpose other than obtaining the tax benefit (but for the provisions of this Chapter),*

without having any regard to –
   (A) *whether or not the funds involved in the round trip financing can be traced to any funds transferred to, or received by, any party in connection with the arrangement;*
   (B) *the time, or sequence, in which the funds involved in the round trip financing are transferred or received; or*
   (C) *the means by, or manner in, or mode through, which funds involved in the round trip financing are transferred or received.*

(3) *For the purposes of this Chapter, a party to an arrangement shall be an accommodating party, if the main purpose of the direct or indirect participation of that party in the arrangement, in whole or in part, is to obtain, directly or indirectly, a tax benefit (but for the provisions of this Chapter) for the assessee whether or not the party is a connected person in relation to any party to the arrangement.*

(4) *For the removal of doubts, it is hereby clarified that the following may be relevant but shall not be sufficient for determining whether an arrangement lacks commercial substance or not, namely: –*
   (i) *the period or time for which the arrangement (including operations therein) exists;*

(ii) the fact of payment of taxes, directly or indirectly, under the arrangement;

(iii) the fact that an exit route (including transfer of any activity or business or operations) is provided by the arrangement

"Consequences of impermissible avoidance arrangement.

98. (1) If an arrangement is declared to be an impermissible avoidance arrangement, then, the consequences, in relation to tax, of the arrangement, including denial of tax benefit or a benefit under a tax treaty, shall be determined, in such manner as is deemed appropriate, in the circumstances of the case, including by way of but not limited to the following, namely: —

- *(a) disregarding, combining or recharacterising any step in, or a part or whole of, the impermissible avoidance arrangement;*
- *(b) treating the impermissible avoidance arrangement as if it had not been entered into or carried out;*
- *(c) disregarding any accommodating party or treating any accommodating party and any other party as one and the same person;*
- *(d) deeming persons who are connected persons in relation to each other to be one and the same person for the purposes of determining tax treatment of any amount;*
- *(e) reallocating amongst the parties to the arrangement —*
  - *(i) any accrual, or receipt, of a capital nature or revenue nature; or*
  - *(ii) any expenditure, deduction, relief or rebate;*
- *(f) treating —*
  - *(i) the place of residence of any party to the arrangement; or*
  - *(ii) the situs of an asset or of a transaction,*

> at a place other than the place of residence, location of the asset or location of the transaction as provided under the arrangement; or
> (g) considering or looking through any arrangement by disregarding any corporate structure.
> (2) For the purposes of sub-section (1), –
> (i) any equity may be treated as debt or vice versa;
> (ii) any accrual, or receipt, of a capital nature may be treated as of revenue nature or vice versa; or
> (iii) (iii) any expenditure, deduction, relief or rebate may be recharacterised.

WITH THE ADVENT OF GENERAL ANTI AVOIDANCE RULES (GAAR), THERE WILL BE A PARADIGM SHIFT IN THE TAXATION REGIME & AGAIN A PANDORA BOX OF LITIGATIONS WILL OPEN UP....

The legislative intent behind the introduction of an altogether new Chapter X-A, containing the GAAR provisions, has been to curb the use of colourable devices facilitating tax evasion. However, a lot of subjectivity had been crept in the manner in which the text of sections 95 to 102, had been drafted. The denial of tax benefit in an impermissible avoidance arrangement aimed at tax evasion, is completely justifiable. However, the most significant and crucial aspect, i.e. what would constitute an impermissible avoidance arrangement, has been left to subjective whims and fancies of the Assessing Authorities.

A plain reading of the above stated GAAR provisions, makes it amply clear, that very wide & unfettered powers have been given to the Assessing Authorities, to completely disregard the legal form of any arrangement/transaction, and to look into the substance of the transaction, to pierce the corporate veil, to treat capital receipts as revenue receipts, and to treat any arrangement as an impermissible avoidance agreement, assuming it to be lacking commercial substance.

In order to put a suitable check on the blatant & adhoc application of the GAAR provisions, which might be widely used, to make exorbitant additions in assessments, suitable amendments must be incorporated in the concerned sections, so as to provide a standard and objective set of determining factors and parameters, with a view to ensure the judicious and rational application of the said provisions, in order to avoid the foreseeable unreasonable and high-handed approach to the assessees. Then only, in true spirit and form, the Governments' objective of ensuring "Ease of Doing Business" will be accomplished.

TAXALOGUE 6

Going for a Date with Assessing Authority for Stay of Demand!!

The month of February is usually associated with love, aspirations and valentine dates. For assessees and their tax consultants also, it do culminates into dates with assessing authorities, (I leave it up to you to think them to be valentine dates or not), as it is that part of the year, when the regular assessments get concluded and the statutory time-limit of 30 days in the demand notices also gets over and the assessing authorities start putting pressure for recovery of income tax demands…..

By virtue of CBDT Office Memorandum dated 31.7.2017, the assessing authorities, as a matter of right, are demanding atleast 20% of the corresponding income tax demands, w.r.t. the assessments, even in cases of High-Pitched Assessments. An assessment is termed as high pitched if the assessed income is twice the returned income or more.

However, whether the assessing authorities, by default, are authorised to demand and collect, atleast 20% of the income tax demand, in all assessment cases? This article tries to address this burning issue having an impact on almost all the assessees and their tax consultants.

It is usual for us to take some tips from our friends before going for valentine dates. So, if you are about to have that valentine date with the assessing authority, who is pre-determined to recover and collect atleast 20% of the income-tax demand, then this article may prove helpful.

It will be in the fitness of things to consider the relevant CBDT Circulars and the related judicial pronouncements having a direct bearing on the issue of stay of grant in high pitched assessment cases.

The First CBDT Instruction addressing the issue of Grant of Stay of Demand in High Pitched Assessments was CBDT Instruction No. 95 dated 21.8.1969. It categorically provided that,

> *"Where the income determined on assessment was substantially higher than the returned income, say twice the latter amount or more, the collection of the tax in dispute should be held in abeyance till the decision on the appeal provided there were no lapses on the part of the assesses."*

Therefore, the said CBDT Instruction, very clearly provided that in case of high- pitched assessments, the tax recovery proceedings should be kept in abeyance and the stay of grant should be provided by the assessing authorities to the assessees, till the disposal of appeal by the appellate authority.

Then CBDT had come up with another Instruction No. 1914 dated 2.12.1993, on Stay of Demand, and the

Revenue Authorities contended that all previous instructions stood superseded by the said instruction, which included the supersession of the earlier CBDT Instruction No. 95 dated 21.8.1969, also.

This matter was the subject matter of consideration in the judgment of the Hon'ble Delhi High Court in the case of *"Taneja Developers and Infrastracture Ltd., Vs. Assistant Commissioner of Income Tax, Delhi and Ors in W.P.(C).No.6956 of 2009, (2009) 222 CTR (Del) 521 dated 24.02.2009,* wherin the Hon'ble Delhi High Court, relying upon its earlier judgment in the case of *"Valvoline Cummins Ltd. v. CIT and Ors. (2008) 217 CTR (Del) 292,* had categorically held as under,

"9.Having considered the arguments advanced by the learned counsel for the parties, we are of the view that although Instruction No.1914 of 1993 specifically states that it is in supersession of all earlier instructions, the position obtaining after the decision of this Court in Valvoline Cummins Ltd., (Supra) is not altered at all. This is so because paragraph No.2(A) which speaks of responsibility specifically indicates that it shall be the responsibility of the Assessing Officer and the TRO to collect every demand that has been raised except the following', which includes: (d) demand stayed in accordance with the paras B and C below. Para B relates to stay petitions. As extracted above, Sub-clause (iii) of para B clearly indicates that a higher/superior authority could interfere with the decision of the Assessing Officer/TRO only in exceptional circumstances. The exceptional circumstances have been indicated as – "where the assessment order appears to be unreasonably

high pitched or where genuine hardship is likely to be caused to the assessee.... The very question as to what would constitute the assessment order as being reasonably high pitched in consideration under the said Instruction No.96 and, there, it has been noted by way of illustration that assessment at twice the amount of the returned income would amount to being substantially higher or high pitched. In the case before this Court in Valvoline Cummins Ltd., (supra) that assessee's income was about eight (8) times the returned income. This Court was of the view that was high pitched. In the present case, the assessed income is approximately 74 times the returned income and obviously, this would fall within the expression unreasonably high pitched. (Emphasis supplied)...

A reading of the above dictum would show that if assessment order is unreasonably high pitched or genuine hardship is likely to be caused to the assessee, then the assessee is entitled to be treated as not being in default in respect of the amount in dispute in the appeal."

Then CBDT had again come up with CBDT Office Memorandum dated 29.2.2016, which provides that a Stay of Demand may be granted to the assessee on deposition of 15% (further increased to 20% by CBDT office memorandum dated 31.7.2017), of the total outstanding income tax demand, if the assessee's appeal is pending before the CIT(Appeals). The assessing authorities, by virtue of the said CBDT Office Memorandums, as a matter of their inherent right, by default, are pressurizing for deposition of atleast 20% of the total income tax demand, even in cases of high-pitched assessments.

However, again the third pillar of democracy, i.e. the Judiciary, has come to the rescue of the assessees.

In a recent judgement of the Hon'ble Karnataka High Court, in the case of *M/s Flipkart India Pvt Ltd vs ACIT, Circle 3(1)(1), vide Writ Petition Nos. 1339-1342/2017 (T-IT), 23.2.2017,* the Hon'ble High Court has categorically held as follows:

Para 16 "*.....It is true that Instruction No.4 (B)(b) of the Circular dated 29.2.2016, gives two instances where less than 15% can be asked to be deposited. However, it is equally true that the factors, which were directed to be kept in mind both by the Assessing Officer, and by the higher superior authority, contained in Instruction No.2-B(iii) of Circular No.1914, still continue to exist. For, as noted above, the said part of Circular No.1914 has been left untouched by the Circular dated 29.2.2016. Therefore, while dealing with an application filed by an assessee, both the Assessing Officer, and the Prl. CIT, are required to see if the assessee's case would fall under Instruction No.2-B(iii) of Circular No.1914, or not? Both the Assessing Officer, and the Prl. CIT, are required to examine whether the assessment is "unreasonably high pitched", or whether the demand for depositing 15% of the disputed demand amount "would lead to a genuine hardship being caused to the assessee" or not?*

The principal ratios emerging from the aforesaid High Court judgments clearly provide that in the cases of high-pitched assessments, the stipulation of blanket deposition of atleast 20% of the income tax demand, is not applicable and stay of demand ought to be granted to the assessees, by the assessing authorities. This is because of the fact that even the deposition of 20% of the exorbitant and arbitrary income-tax demand in high pitched assessment cases, would result in a lot of financial and other hardships to the assessees and would also make the right of their appeal totally meaningless and nugatory.

Before parting, one more useful suggestion…. In case of High Pitched Assessment Cases, i.e. where assessed income is twice the returned income or more, an Application for Granting Appropriate Relief in terms of Absolute Stay of Demand and Early Fixation of Appeal, may be filed before the "High Pitched Assessment Grievance Committee" headed by the Jurisdictional Principal Chief Commissioner of Income Tax, of that region.

SO, FRIENDS, NOW GO FOR THAT VALENTINE DATE WITH YOUR ASSESSING OFFICER, FOR STAY OF DEMAND, MUCH MORE CONFIDENTLY AND BACKED UP WITH LEGAL PRECEDENTS. ALL THE BEST...

TAXALOGUE 7

Charitable Trusts: Income Tax Perspective

"Charity begins at home but should not end there." – Francis Bacon

The essence of the above quote has been fully captured in the definition of the expression "charitable purpose" as envisaged in the Income Tax Act, 1961.

Under the Indian Income Taxation Laws, a trust is considered as charitable, if its objects are directed to the benefit of the society at large and not for an individual or group of individuals.

More specifically section 2(15) of the Income Tax Act, 1961, defines the expression "charitable purpose" as under:

Section 2(15): *"charitable purpose" includes relief of the poor, education, yoga, medical relief, preservation of environment (including watersheds, forests and wildlife) and preservation of monuments or places or objects of artistic or historic interest, and the advancement of any other object of general public utility:*

Provided that the advancement of any other object of general public utility shall not be a charitable purpose, if it involves the carrying on of any activity in the nature of trade, commerce or business, or any activity of rendering any service in relation to any trade, commerce or business, for a cess or fee or any other consideration, irrespective of the nature of use or application, or retention, of the income from such activity, unless—

(i) such activity is undertaken in the course of actual carrying out of such advancement of any other object of general public utility; and

(ii) the aggregate receipts from such activity or activities during the previous year, do not exceed twenty per cent of the total receipts, of the trust or institution undertaking such activity or activities, of that previous year;

Owing to its aim of social development of the country, charitable trusts have received favoured and preferential treatment in the Indian Taxation Laws, since 1886.

The taxation of charitable trusts is governed by Chapter III of the Income Tax Act which contains sections 11, 12, 12A, 12AA and 13.

Section 12A/12AA contains the provisions concerning the Registration and the Registration Procedure under the Income Tax Act. Section 11 and 12 contains the provisions concerning the conditions to be fulfilled by the charitable trusts in order to claim exemption from income tax. Section 13 stipulates the provisions concerning the trusts which are not eligible for exemption u/s 11 & 12.

Conditions for applicability of sec 11 and 12

In order to secure exemption u/s 11, the property must be held under trust, besides section 12A lays down that the exemption under section 11 and 12, shall not be available unless the following conditions are fulfilled:

(a) Registration: The trust is required to obtain registration u/s 12AA with the Commissioner of Income-tax.

(b) Compulsory Audit: Where the total income of the trust or institution, exceeds the basic exemption limit, that is, Rs.2, 50,000/- in any previous year, the accounts of the trust or institution is required to be audited by a qualified Chartered Accountant, and the audit report in Form No. 10B is required to be furnished electronically before filing the e-return of income.

Filing of Return Sec 139(4A)

Where the total income of the trust (before allowing exemption under sections 11 and 12) exceeds the maximum amounts which is not chargeable to tax (i.e. Rs.2,50,000 for A.Y.2015-16 and onwards), it is required to file its return in Form ITR-7, before the date specified in section 139. The due date specified under section 139 is 30th September every year where the trust is required to get its accounts audited under any provision of the Act and 31st July every year in other case.

In case return is not filed by prescribed date then benefit of accumulation u/s 11(2) will not be available. [sec 13(9) inserted w.e.f. 1.4.2016]

Income Applied to Charitable or Religious Purposes [Sec 11(1)]

Section 11(1) of the Income Tax lays down that any income, profits and gains derived from property held under trust wholly for religious and charitable purposes, (or held in part only for such purposes-in case of trust created before 1/4/1962) shall not be included in the total income of the trust or institution (including a society or any other legal obligation) to the extent such income is applied or accumulated for application to such purposes. The exemption is, allowable under specified circumstances, on fulfillment of certain conditions.

In order to be eligible for claiming exemption, it is essential that the income of the trust is applied to such objects. A charitable trust or institution will have to apply at least 85 % of the income to charitable purposes. If the income spent on charitable or religious purposes, during the previous year, falls short of 85 % of the income derived during the year, such shortfall will be liable to tax. Voluntary contribution or donations (not being contributions made with a specific direction that they will form part of the corpus) will be deemed to be a part of income derived from property held under trust.

Exemption for Accumulation of Income in Excess of Specified Limit [Sec 11(2)]

Where 85% of income derived from trust property is not applied or is not deemed to have been applied for charitable purposes, but is accumulated or set apart for application for such purposes in India, exemption can be claimed for the income so accumulated or set apart in excess of 15% limit, provided the following conditions are complied with:

(a) a statement in form 10B to be uploaded electronically within the time allowed for furnishing the return u/s 139(1), notifying the amount being accumulated and the period of accumulation. In case form no. 10B is not uploaded before this date then the benefit of accumulation will not be available and such income will be taxable at appropriate rate.

(b) the period of accumulation does not exceed 5 years and

(c) the money so accumulated is invested or deposited in modes or forms specified u/s 11(5).

(d) From A.Y.2016-17 benefit of accumulation is not available if return of income is not furnished before due date of filing return as per Sec 139(1).

Are Charitable Trusts allowed to carry forward their losses/deficits of the earlier years for setoff against their incomes of subsequent years?

Till very recently, the Revenue Authorities were very consistently disallowing the charitable trusts' claim of carry forward of their losses/deficits of the earlier years for setoff against their incomes of subsequent years, and thus such deficits were considered as dead losses.

However, the issue of allowability of the claim of loss u/s 11 and carry forward of the same to subsequent year to be set off against incomes of subsequent years by the charitable trusts is **no longer** *"Res Intigra"* as the **Hon'ble Supreme Court** in the case of *"CIT(Exemptions) vs. Subros Educational Society"* (2018) 303 CTR 1 / 166 DTR 257 (SC), have upheld the judgement of the jurisdictional Hon'ble Delhi High Court, in the same case reported in IT No. 382 of 2015 dated 23.9.2015, and have categorically dismissed the SLP being filed by the Revenue Authorities against the said judgement.

In the said judgement the Hon'ble Supreme Court have categorically answered the following question of law in AFFIRMATIVE, viz.

"Whether any excess expenditure incurred by the trust/charitable institution in earlier assessment year could be allowed to be set off against income of

subsequent years by invoking Section 11 of the Income Tax Act, 1961?"

Therefore, in view of the binding judgement of the Hon'ble Supreme Court in the case of *"CIT(Exemptions) vs. Subros Educational Society"* (2018) 303 CTR 1 / 166 DTR 257 (SC), as above, the issue of allowability of the claim of loss u/s 11 and carry forward of the same to subsequent year to be set off against incomes of subsequent years by the charitable trusts, has attained finality in favour of charitable trusts assessees and as such from now onwards, there should not be any question of any disallowance in this regards, by the ld. Assessing Authority.

Corpus Donations towards Corpus Funds are fully exempt and there is no requirement of fulfilment of the stipulated criteria of application of atleast 85% for such Corpus Donations [Sec 11(1)(d)]

Corpus donations refer to the donations made by a donor to a trust with a specific direction that they shall form part of the corpus of the recipient trust. The donor alone can give a specific direction that the donation made by him shall form part of the corpus of the trust. Trustees have no power to treat in their discretion any donation as corpus donation. Such direction may preferably be given by the donor in writing by a letter addressed to the trust. If he has not done so, trustees may request him to give such directions in writing. If any contribution is made with a specific direction, that it shall be treated as the capital of the trust for carrying out a particular charitable activity, it satisfies the definition part of the corpus.

Corpus donations being capital receipt in the hands of the recipient trust are not income of the trust. Section 11(1)(d) expressly grants exemption to corpus donations Contributions to corpus fund kept in fixed deposit cannot be taxed as income even if corpus fund is misused -CIT v Sri Durga Nimishambha Trust [2012] 205 Taxman 59 (Mag) (Kar).

The corpus would include funds of a capital nature, by whatever name called, such as Building Fund, as well as funds for capital expenditure of the trust. Any donation made for a capital purpose or with a direction that donation be kept intact and only the interest received on the investment of such donation be utilized for the objects of the trust, would be a donation towards the corpus of the trust.

Corpus donations may not be applied to charitable purposes and these may be retained as forming part of the corpus of the trust without attracting any tax liability in the matter. The trustees must however utilize the income accruing from the corpus for charitable purposes of the trust.

Withdrawal of Exemption granted to Income accumulated u/s 11(2)

The income which is accumulated or set apart in accordance with the provision of Section 11(2), shall become taxable if-

(a) It is applied to purpose other than charitable or religious purposes;

(b) It ceases to remain invested in the specified form or modes of deposit; or

(c) It is not utilized for charitable or religious purposes within the specified accumulation period (which shall not exceed 10 years/5 years in respect of income accumulated on or after 1.4.2001); or

(d) It is paid or credited to any trust/institution registered u/s12AA or to any fund/institution/trust/university/other educational institution/hospital/any other medical institution referred to in clauses (iv), (v), (vi), and (via) of Section 10(23C).

Under any of the aforesaid circumstances, the amount involved shall be deemed to be income of the previous year in which it is so misapplied or ceases to be so accumulated or ceases to remain invested or is credited or paid or the previous year immediately following the expiry of the specified accumulation period, as the case may be. **[Sec 11(3)]**.

Charitable Trust Carrying on a Business [Sec 11(4) & 11(4A)]

"Benevolence today has become altogether too huge an undertaking to be conducted otherwise than on business lines." -Julius Rosenwald

There is no prohibition on a charitable trust carrying on a business. A charitable trust can be settled in relation to any property including a business undertaking. The income from such business shall also qualify for exemption provided the other conditions of sections11 and 12 are fulfilled.

The income of such business shall be determined in accordance with the provisions of the Act. i.e Section 28 to 44 DB. Where the income from such business as determined by the Assessing Officer is found to be in excess of the income shown in the accounts, then such excess shall be deemed to have been applied to non-charitable or non-religious purposes and such excess income shall not qualify for exemption. **As per sec 11(4)** income of any business held in trust for charitable purpose shall be eligible for exemption.

Further, any income of a trust being profits and gains of business, shall not qualify for exemption unless the business is incidental to the attainment of the objects of the trust and separate books of account are maintained in respect of such business as per Sec **11(4A)**.

The Supreme Court in the case of Asst. CIT vs. **Thanthi Trust** (2001) 247 ITR 785 (SC) has held that all that is required for the business income of a trust or institution to be exempt from tax is that the business should be incidental to the attainment of objective of the trust or institution. A business whose income is utilised by the trust or the institution for the purposes of achieving the objectives of the trust or the institution is a business which is incidental to the attainment of the objectives of the trust or institution.

Thus, in determining whether the trust is entitled to exemption u/s 11, the nature or type of the sources of income of the trust is not relevant. What is necessary to be considered is whether having regard to all the facts and circumstances of the case, the dominant object of the activity is profit-making or carrying out a charitable purpose. This involves, in each case an examination of not only the objects of the trust but also the manner in which the activities for advancing the charitable purpose are being carried on and the surrounding circumstances. Hon'ble Supreme Court in the case of DIT vs. **Bharat Diamond Bourse** (2003) 126 Taxman 365 (SC) has held that if the primary or dominant purpose of the institution is charitable and another which by itself, may not be charitable, but is merely ancillary or incidental to the primary or dominant object, it would not prevent the institution from validly being recognized as a charity. The test to be applied is, whether the object which is said to be non- charitable is the main or primary object of the trust or institution or it is ancillary or incidental to the dominant object which is charitable.

Exemption in relation to capital gains [Sec 11(1A)].

The amount of exemption in relation to capital gains arising on transfer of a capital asset of charitable trusts shall be as under:

i. Where the capital asset is held under trust wholly for charitable or religious purposes:

a. If the whole of the net consideration is utilised for acquisition of a new capital asset, the entire capital gain shall be exempt; and

b. if only a part of the net consideration is so utilized, the amount of capital gain exempt shall be equal to -

Cost of Acquisition of the New Capital Asset Minus Cost of Capital Asset Transferred

ii. Where the capital asset is held under trust in part only for charitable or religious purposes:

a. if the whole of the net consideration is utilized for acquisition of new capital asset, the amount of capital gain exempt shall be equal to,

(A/B * Total Capital Gain)

b. if only a part of the net consideration is so utilized, the amount of capital gain exempt, shall be equal to,

c. [A/B * (Cost of Acquisition - A/B * (Cost of Capital Of New Capital Asset) Asset Transferred)]

Where

A= Income derived from the capital asset transferred and applied to charitable or religious purpose, before its transfer,

B= Total income derived from the capital asset before its transfer.

Explanatory Notes: -

(i) Cost of Capital Asset Transferred means the aggregate of cost of acquisition of the asset and cost of any improvement thereto. In case of long-term capital assets, the indexed cost of acquisition and indexed cost improvement shall be considered.

(ii) Net consideration means= full value of consideration less expenses in connection with transfer.

(iii) Capital Gains to be calculated as per applicable provisions of the Act.

New Capital Asset – Whether includes Fixed Deposit?

While examining this question, the Board had clarified that investment of the net consideration in fixed deposit with a Bank for a period of 6 months or above would be regarded as utilization of the net consideration for acquisition of another capital asset within the meaning of section 11(1A) [Vide CBDT's Instruction No:883 dated 24.9.1975, Taxman's Direct Taxes Circular 1994 Ed. Vol. I, page 1.326].

In **CIT vs. East India Charitable Trust** (1994) 2016 ITR 152, the Calcutta High Court has held that in view of section 11(5)(vii), deposits with public sector companies, shall qualify as 'new capital asset' within the meaning of section 11(1A).

It is pertinent to mention here that the charitable trusts have an option to either claim specific exemption u/s 11(1A) in relation to the capital gains or to claim general exemption u/s 11(1)(a) by applying atleast 85% of the total income including the sale proceeds of sold capital assets towards their charitable objectives.

Trusts Not Eligible for Exemption [Sec 13]

Following trusts are not eligible for exemption under Section 11 and 12:

(a) A trust for private religious purposes, which ensures no public benefit: **[Sec 13(1)(a)]**

(b) A charitable trust created or established on or after 1.4.1962 for the benefit of any particular religious community or caste **[Sec 13(1)(b)]** (other than scheduled castes/tribes, back-ward classes or women and children). (Explanation 2)

(c) A trust or institution for charitable or religious purposes, if any part of its income or property is used or applied, or enure, directly or indirectly for the benefit of a person specified u/s 13(3) viz.(i) the author or founder of the trust ; (ii) a substantial contributor whose total contributions to the trust upto the end of the relevant previous year exceed Rs.50,000; (iii) where the author or contributor is an HUF, a member of the family; (iv) the trustee or manger of the trust; (v) any relative of such author, founder, contributor, member, trustee or manager; and (vi) any concern in which any of the persons aforesaid has a substantial interest. **[Sec 13(1)(c)]**

When Application of Funds deemed to have been made for the benefit of specified Persons- [Sec 13(2)]

Applications of the trust-income or the trust-property for the following purposes is deemed to have been made for the benefit of specified persons.

(a) If a loan is given to a specified person for any period during the previous year without either adequate security or adequate interest or both;

(b) If any land, building or other property of the trust, is allowed to be utilized by a specified person, without charging adequate rent or other compensation:

(c) If payment is made by way of salary, allowance, etc. to a specified person for services rendered by him to the trust or institution, in excess of what may be reasonably paid for such services;

(d) If the trust renders its services to a specified person without adequate remuneration or other compensation; (Exception Medical/Educational Institution)

(e) If any share, security or other property is transferred to the trust from a specified person, for a consideration which is more than adequate;

(f) If any share, security or other property is transferred by the trust to a specified person, for inadequate consideration;

(g) If any income or property of the trust, exceeding Rs. 1000 in value, is diverted to a specified person; and

(h) If the trust-funds are invested, or remain invested, for any period in any concern wherein any of the specified persons has a substantial interest.[Sec 13(2)]

Recent Amendments incorporated by Legislature:

"My business is the enforcement of the tax laws and the integrity of the tax code and making sure that trustees of charitable giving are true trustees."-Chuck Grassley

With instances of misuse of funds by trusts owned by corporate entities, the Government is continuously tightening the law to bring more transparency in the working of charitable trusts. Some of the prominent amendments being incorporated by the Legislature in this regard are listed as under:

1) Levy of tax at the maximum marginal rate where a charitable trust ceases to exist or converts into a non-charitable entity (Secs.115 TD to 115 TF) inserted wef- 1.6.2016

Section 11 and 12 provide for exemption to trusts or institution in respect of income derived from property held under trust and voluntary contributions, subject to various conditions contained in the said sections. A charitable trust may voluntarily wind up its activities and dissolve or may also merge with any other non-charitable institution, or to may convert into a non - charitable organisation. Moreover, it is always possible for charitable institutions to transfer assets to a non-charitable institution. In such cases, the existing law does not provide for an clarity as to how the assets of such a charitable institution shall be charged to tax.

In order to ensure that the benefit conferred over the years to charitable trust is not misused, section 115 TD is inserted with effect from June 1, 2016. This section provides for levy of additional income –tax in case of conversion into, or merger with, any non- charitable form or on transfer of assets of a charitable organisation on its dissolution to a non-charitable institution. The elements of the regime are-

Time of accreted income – The accretion in income (accreted income) of the trust or institution shall be taxable on-

Conversion of trust or institution into a from not eligible for registration under section 12 AA; or

Merger into an entity not having similar objects and which is not registered under section 12 AA; or

Non –distribution of assets on dissolution to any charitable institution registered under section 12AA or approved under section 10(23C) within a period of 12 months for dissolution.

• **Deemed conversion** – For the above purpose, a trust or institution shall be deemed to have been converted into any from (not eligible for registration under section 12 AA) in a previous year, if-

-The registration granted to it under section 12AA has been cancelled; or

-It has modified its objects and not applied for fresh registration (or fresh registration application has been rejected).

Meaning of accreted income – Accreted income shall be amount of aggregate of fair market value of total assets as reduced by the liability as on the specified date (i.e., the date of conversion, merger or dissolution). Mode of valuation to be notified.

Exclusions from accreted income – So much of the accreted income as is attributable to the following asset and liability, if any, related to such asset shall be ignored for the purpose of computation of accreted income –

a. Any asset which is established to have been directly acquired be the trust or institution out of agricultural income as is referred to in section 10 (1).

b. Any asset acquired by the trust/institution during the period beginning from the date of its creation and ending on the date from which the registration under section 12 AA became effective or deemed effective (however, this rule is valid only if the trust/ institution has not been allowed any benefit of sections 11 and 12 during the said period). "Deemed " effective covers a case where due to first proviso to section 12 A (2) the benefit of section 11 and 12 have been allowed to the trust/ institution in respect of any previous year prior to the year of registration.

- Further, the asset and the liability of the charitable organisation, which have been transferred to another charitable organisation within specified time, will be excluded while calculation accreted income.

Tax liability – The taxation of accreted income shall be at the maximum marginal rate (i.e.35.535 per cent for the assessment year 2017-18).

This levy shall be in addition to any income chargeable to tax in the hands of the entity and this tax shall be final tax for which no credit can be taken by the trust or institution or any other person, and like any other additional tax, it shall be leviable even if the trust or institution does not have any other income chargeable to tax in the relevant previous year.

2) Mandatory Requirement of obtaining PAN for the Trustees: Section 139A is amended to the effect that every person, not being an individual, which enters into a financial transaction of an amount aggregating to two lakh and fifty thousand rupees or more in a financial year shall be required to apply to the Assessing Officer for allotment of PAN. This is done in order to use PAN as Unique Entity Number (UEN) for non-individual entities.

It is also provided that the trustee, author, founder, chief executive officer, principal officer or office-bearer or any person competent to act on behalf of such entities shall also apply to the Assessing Officer for allotment of PAN.

This is done in order to link the financial transactions with the natural persons.

3) Mandatory Requirement of TDS Deduction:

At present:

- There are no checks on whether such trusts or institutions follow the provisions of deduction of tax at source under Chapter XVII-B of the Act.

- This has led to lack of an audit trail for verification of application of income.

Section 11 provides for exemption in respect of income derived from property held under trust for charitable or religious purposes to the extent to which such income is applied or accumulated during the previous year for certain purposes in accordance with the relevant provisions.

A new *Explanation* to the said section has been inserted so as to provide that for the purposes of determining the amount of application under clause (*a*) or clause (*b*) of sub-section (1) thereof, the provisions of sub-clause (*ia*) of clause (*a*) of section 40 and sub-sections (3) and (3A) of section 40A, shall, *mutatis mutandis*, apply as they apply in computing the income chargeable under the head "Profits and gains of business or profession".

Non-deduction of tax at source would now attract disallowance in the hands of the charitable trust also. Thus, now trusts will be mandatorily required to deduct TDS as per provisions of Chapter XVII-B of the Act to claim expense as the application of Income. Else the same will be taxable in the hands of Trusts.

4) Disallowance of Expenditure Exceeding Rs. 10,000/- in Cash:

The provisions of section 40(3) and 40(3A) will be mutatis mutandis apply to the Trusts. Earlier, charitable trusts were availing benefits even in respect of the application of income by way of cash payments. This amendment is again in line with the dream of digital India and cashless economy.

Thus, payment exceeding Rs. 10,000 in cash will not be considered as the application of income and the same will be taxable in the hands of trusts.

5) Maximum Limit of Cash Donations reduced from Rs. 10,000/- to Rs. 2,000/-

Restrictions have been imposed on cash donations of the charitable trusts under section 80G by reducing the capping from Rs. 10,000 to Rs. 2,000. This is to ensure that unaccounted money does not flow into the charitable institutions in the form of anonymous donations.

6). Power of Survey u/s 133A: Giving more powers to the tax authorities, it has been provided that now the income tax officers can conduct surveys under section 133A on trustees and places of activity for charitable purpose.

7) Section 35AC which allowed 100% tax deduction to individuals and companies making contributions to specific charitable organizations for specific schemes, shall no longer be available to donors starting April 1, 2017.

Conclusion: The very rationale of providing tax incentives and exemptions to charitable trusts is to encourage them to render public service and not to accumulate tax-free wealth in the disguise of social service. The Taxation Laws concerning charitable trusts have evolved over a period of time. The recent amendments as incorporated by the Legislature will definitely prevent abuse of tax exemptions and improve tax administration in relation to the charitable trusts.

"Do your little bit of good where you are; it's those little bits of good put together that overwhelm the world." - Desmond Tutu

TAXALOGUE 8

Tata's Six Charitable Trusts' Registration: Cancellation or Voluntary Surrender?

In tax assessments of high-profile cases, disruption in the *'status quo'* always garners public attention and brings with it, a whole new interesting and intriguing dimension to the otherwise routine tax practice and legal jurisprudence.

The recent cancellation of the Tata's Six Charitable Trusts' Registration by the Office of the PCIT Mumbai on October 31, 2019 is one such disruption, which has definitely caused tremors and vibrations in the tax circles, and has caught the attention and limelight in all the national dailies and print media.

The six Tata trusts, the registrations of which have been cancelled by the Revenue Authorities are Sir Dorabji Tata Trust, Sir Ratan Tata Trust, JRD Tata Trust, Tata Education Trust, Tata Social Welfare Trust and Sarvajanik Seva Trust.

Interestingly, the cancellation of the registration of these six charitable trusts is not the debatable and litigative issue here but the date from which the said cancellation has to be considered as operative and effective in law, is the main bone of contention between the Income-tax department and the Tata Group.

The Revenue Authorities are contending that the trusts' registration as charitable organisations ought to be cancelled from the date of passing of the registration cancellation order dated 31.10.2019, whereas the Tata Trusts' plea is the admissibility of voluntary surrender of the charitable status by these six trusts in the year 2015 only.

So, one would wonder as to why there is so much fuss about the effective date of cancellation of these trusts' registrations when the Tata Group is in agreement with the closure of the charitable status of these six trusts and infact had suo-motto surrendered the registration of these six trusts in the year 2015 itself.

The moot question in point is the applicability or otherwise of section 115TD of the Income Tax Act, to these six trusts, and the consequential huge income-tax liability on the accreted income of these six trusts.

What does section 115TD of the Income Tax Act says?

According to Section 115TD of the Income Tax Act, a trust whose registration is cancelled is required to pay tax on its accumulated or 'accreted' income.

In order to ensure that the benefit conferred over the years to a charitable trust by way of exemption of its income u/s 11, is not being misused, section 115TD has been inserted with effect from June 1, 2016. This section provides for levy of additional income-tax on the accreted income of the charitable trust in case of its winding up, or conversion into, or merger with any non-charitable form or on transfer of assets of a charitable trust on its dissolution to a non-charitable institution.

Time of accreted income – The accretion in income (accreted income) of the trust or institution shall be taxable on-

- Conversion of trust or institution into a from not eligible for registration under section 12 AA; or
- Merger into an entity not having similar objects and which is not registered under section 12 AA; or
- Non-distribution of assets on dissolution to any charitable institution registered under section 12AA or approved under section 10(23C) within a period of 12 months for dissolution.

Deemed conversion – For the above purpose, a trust or institution shall be deemed to have been converted into any from (not eligible for registration under section 12AA) in a previous year, if-

- **The registration granted to it under section 12AA has been cancelled**; or

- It has modified its objects and not applied for fresh registration (or fresh registration application has been rejected).

Meaning of accreted income – Accreted income shall be the amount of aggregate of fair market value of total assets as reduced by the liability as on the specified date (i.e., the date of conversion, merger or dissolution).

Exclusions from accreted income – So much of the accreted income as is attributable to the undermentioned assets and liabilities, if any, related to such assets shall be ignored for the purpose of computation of accreted income:

a. Any asset which is established to have been directly acquired be the trust or institution out of agricultural income as is referred to in section 10 (1).

b. Any asset acquired by the trust/institution during the period beginning from the date of its creation and ending on the date from which the registration under section 12 AA became effective or deemed effective (however , this rule is valid only if the trust/ institution has not been allowed any benefit of sections 11 and 12 during the said period). "Deemed "effective covers a case where due to first proviso to section 12 A(2), the benefit of section 11 and 12 have been allowed to the trust/ institution in respect of any previous year prior to the year of registration.

Further, the assets and the liabilities of the charitable trust, which have been transferred to another charitable trust within specified time, will be excluded while calculation accreted income.

Tax liability u/s 115TD: The taxation of accreted income shall be at the maximum marginal rate (i.e.35.535 per cent for the assessment year 2017-18 and onwards).

This levy shall be in addition to any income chargeable to tax in the hands of the entity and this tax shall be final tax for which no credit can be taken by the trust or institution or any other person, and like any other additional tax, it shall be leviable even if the trust or institution does not have any other income chargeable to tax in the relevant previous year.

Backdrop of the Present Cases of these Six Tata Trusts:

In July 2019, the I-T department has served notices on these six Tata Trusts, seeking to reopen their assessments on the basis of alleged irregularities in the modes of making investments in shares of Tata Group concerns by these trusts and questioning the legal validity of voluntary surrender of their registrations in the year 2015 after being found guilty of these contraventions. These re-assessment proceedings have been concluded vide re-assessment orders dated 31.10.2019, wherein the registrations of these trusts have been cancelled w.e.f. 31.10.2019 and the tax liability on accreted income u/s 115TD of the Act is being determined on a rough estimate of Rs. 12000 crores.

As per several media reports and National dailies, the dispute dates back to the year 2013, when the Comptroller and Auditor General of India (CAG) pointed out that Jamshedji Tata Trust and Navajbai Ratan Tata Trust had invested Rs 3,139 crore in prohibited modes of investment. The CAG noted that the I-T department had given irregular tax exemptions to these trusts, resulting in atleast Rs 1,066 crore escaping the tax net.

The CAG report said some of the Tata trusts held shares of Tata Consultancy Services (TCS) and Tata Capital Ltd. A part of the TCS shares were subsequently divested and proceeds invested in preference shares of Tata Sons Ltd. These actions, as per the CAG, violated norms governing investments by charitable trusts. These six Tata Trusts, together hold the majority 66% equity stake in Tata Sons Ltd.

In March 2015, the Tata Trusts surrendered their registrations u/s 12AA of the I-T Act while admitting that some of their assets were not in compliance with the provisions of Section 13(1)(d) of the Act. However, following the CAG's observations and subsequent remarks by a sub-panel of the Public Accounts Committee (PAC) in 2018, the matter was transferred to the I-T department's assessment wing from the exemption wing that has now sought an explanation from the trusts by reopening their assessments. The trusts, according to the PAC report, were investing in prohibited modes of investment despite the law strictly forbidding public charitable trusts from holding such assets after 1973.

The Revenue Authorities have 'refused' to accept the Trusts' contention that the cancellation should be with effect from 2015 and have cancelled their registration w.e.f. 31.10.2019 instead and have also pressed into service the provisions of Section 115TD to levy tax on their accreted income.

The Revenue Authorities have cited two main grounds for cancelling registrations of the trusts. One is the investments by the trusts in shares of group companies, which has been prohibited since 1973 u/s 13(1)(d) of the I-T Act. The second is that the trusts were not functioning as per the terms of their deeds.

On the other hand, these six Tata Trusts have contended that with reference to shares of TCS and Tata Capital held by these Trusts, the provisions of Section 13(1)(d) of the

I-T Act would not be applicable as these shares were received by the Trusts as corpus donations and no investments has been made by these Trusts. The investment in preference shares of Tata Sons Ltd was with the permission of the jurisdictional Commissioner of Income-tax and the same were redeemed in May 2016. The proceeds from the redemption flowed into the Trusts' corpus. As per the contention of these six Trusts, Tata Sons Ltd. had agreed to give the higher dividend rate specifically because the Trusts were public charitable trusts. So, the Trusts have infact benefited from the investment. There is nothing to demonstrate that this investment was not in the interest of the Trusts or to suggest that the Trusts could have yielded higher return with any alternative investments.

Another major ground for cancellation of the registrations cited by the I-T department is the alleged violation of the Trusts' deeds. In its show-cause notice, the department has mentioned that the trusts have failed to abide by their own trust deeds as the activities of the trusts are not being carried out in accordance with the objects of the trusts.

The Tata Trusts have refuted this ground also, stating that the I-T department has made general and vague allegations, and has failed to specify the exact activities that were not in accordance with the objects of the Trusts.

Analysis of the Legal Provisions:

The above-stated factual matrix in the cases of these six Tata Trusts makes it clear that the entire thrust of the Income Tax Department's action of cancellation of the registration of these trusts is based purely on the irregularities flagged off by the CAG and the Parliament's Public Accounts Committee (PAC) concerning the alleged irregularities concerning the investments by these Trusts' in the Tata group concerns which are prohibited modes of investments as per provisions of section 13(1)(d) of the I-T Act.

Thus, it is but natural and desirable to consider the provisions of section 13(1)(d) of the Income-tax Act which provides as under:

"13. (1) Nothing contained in section 11 or section 12 shall operate so as to exclude from the total income of the previous year of the person in receipt thereof—

(d) in the case of a trust for charitable or religious purposes or a charitable or religious institution, any income thereof, if for any period during the previous year —

(i) any funds of the trust or institution are invested or deposited after the 28th day of February, 1983 otherwise than in any one or more of the forms or modes specified in sub-section (5) of section 11; or

(ii) any funds of the trust or institution invested or deposited before the 1st day of March, 1983 otherwise than in any one or more of the forms or modes specified in sub-section (5) of section 11 continue to remain so invested or deposited after the 30th day of November, 1983; or

(iii) any shares in a company, other than—

(A) shares in a public sector company;

(B) shares prescribed as a form or mode of investment under clause (xii) of sub-section (5) of section 11,

are held by the trust or institution after the 30th day of November, 1983:

Provided that nothing in this clause shall apply in relation to—

(i) any assets held by the trust or institution where such assets form part of the corpus of the trust or institution as on the 1st day of June, 1973;

Thus, it is duly evident from the above legal provisions of section 13(1)(d)(iii) that the exemption in relation to income u/s 11 shall not be available to a charitable trust if it invests in any shares of a company other than a public sector company, except in the case of such investments forming the part of the corpus of trust since 1.6.1973,

Is the Registration of a Charitable Trust can be Cancelled on account of prohibited modes of Investments as per provisions of section 13(1)(d) of the I-T Act?

(i) Legal Position uptill 30.09.2014

Uptill 30.9.2014, the registration of a charitable trust could be cancelled only as per provisions of section 12AA(3) of the Income-tax Act, which provides as under:

Section 12AA(3): *"Where a trust or an institution has been granted registration under clause (b) of sub-section (1) or has obtained registration at any time under section 12A [as it stood before its amendment by the Finance (No. 2) Act, 1996 (33 of 1996)] and subsequently the Principal Commissioner or Commissioner is satisfied that the activities of such trust or institution are not genuine or are not being carried out in accordance with the objects of the trust or institution, as the case may be, he shall pass an order in writing cancelling the registration of such trust or institution:*

Provided *that no order under this sub-section shall be passed unless such trust or institution has been given a reasonable opportunity of being heard."*

Thus, a plain reading of the above legal provision of section 12AA(3) which was the only enabling provision uptill 30.9.2014 to cancel the registration of a charitable trust, makes it clear that the registration of a charitable trust could be cancelled only if the PCIT was satisfied that the activities of such trust or institution were not genuine or were not being carried out in accordance with the objects of the trust or institution.

There was no reference to section 13(1)(d) in section 12AA(3) and as such the fact of making of investments by the charitable trusts in the prohibited modes other than as provided u/s 11(5) of the I-T Act or in the shares of any company other than a public sector company, as per the provisions of section 13(1)(d) of the Act, can't be made a lawful ground to cancel the registration of such trusts.

So, uptill 30.9.2014, the implication of the applicability of the provisions of section 13(1)(d) of the I-T Act was the denial of exemption of income u/s 11 to the trust and not the cancellation of the trust's registration.

Infact, in several judicial pronouncements and legal precedents it has been held that exemption in respect of only that particular income of the trust can be denied which is in relation to the prohibited modes of investments and exemption u/s 11 in respect of other income having no relation with the prohibited modes of investments, can't be denied to the charitable trust.

In the judgement of the Hon'ble Karnataka High Court, in the case of *CIT Vs Fr. Mullers Charitable Institutions [2014] 44 taxmann.com 275 (Karnataka)*, it was held that perusal of section 13(1)(d) of the Act makes it clear that it is only the income from such investment or deposit, which has been made in violation of section 11(5) of the Act, that is liable to be taxed and violation of section 13(1)(d) does not result in denial of exemption under section 11 to the total income of the assessee trust.

The aforesaid judgement of Karnataka High Court was based on the judgement of Hon'ble Bombay High Court, in the case of *DIT(E) vs. Sheth Mafatlal Gagalbhai Foundation Trust [2001] 114 Taxman 19 (Bombay).*

Interestingly, in the case of one of these six Tata trusts namely *Jamsetji Tata Trust Vs JDIT (E) [2014] 101 DTR (Trib) 305 (Mum)*, the Hon'ble Mumbai Tribunal held that violation of section 13(1)(d) and section 13(2)(h) deprives exemption only to the income from investments not permitted under section 11(5) and not to the entire income of the trust, if the other income of the trust, otherwise fulfils the condition for exemption.

Legal Position w.e.f. 1.10.2014

In order to plug the above lacunae, a new subsection (4) in section 12AA was inserted by the Finance Act, 2014 w.e.f. 01.10.2014. This sub-section (4) of section 12AA has expanded the scope for cancellation of registration of a charitable trust by the Commissioner.

In fact, the situation sought to be covered by section 12AA(4) of the Act revolves around the manner in which activities are carried out, including a case where the income or property of the trust is applied for specific persons like author of trust, trustees, etc; or investment of funds in prohibited modes, etc. The aforesaid are areas, which are contained in section 13 of the Act, which disentitles an assessee from the exemptions contained in section 11 and 12 of the Act.

In other words, violation of section 13 of the Act is also sought to be covered by the Legislature by insertion of sub-section (4) to section 12AA of the Act as a ground for cancellation of registration. However, the said provision is effective only from 01.10.2014.

For ready reference, the provisions of section 12AA(4) of the I-T Act are being reproduced as under:

Section 12AA(4)

"Without prejudice to the provisions of sub-section (3), where a trust or an institution has been granted registration under clause (b) of sub-section (1) or has obtained registration at any time under section 12A [as it stood before its amendment by the Finance (No. 2) Act, 1996 (33 of 1996)] and subsequently it is noticed that

(a) the activities of the trust or the institution are being carried out in a manner that the provisions of sections 11 and 12 do not apply to exclude either whole or any part of the income of such trust or institution due to operation of sub-section (1) of section 13; or

(b) the trust or institution has not complied with the requirement of any other law, as referred to in sub-clause (ii) of clause (a) of sub-section (1), and the order, direction or decree, by whatever name called, holding that such non-compliance has occurred, has either not been disputed or has attained finality,

then, the Principal Commissioner or the Commissioner may, by an order in writing, cancel the registration of such trust or institution:

***Provided** that the registration shall not be cancelled under this sub-section, if the trust or institution proves that there was a reasonable cause for the activities to be carried out in the said manner."*

Application of the above legal provisions in the present case of the six Tata Trusts:

As has already been stated above that the CAG has pointed out in its Audit Report in the year 2013 that Jamshedji Tata Trust and Navajbai Ratan Tata Trust had invested Rs 3,139 crore in prohibited modes of investment and that the I-T department had given irregular tax exemptions to these trusts, resulting in atleast Rs 1,066 crore escaping the tax net.

In March 2015, the six Tata Trusts suo-motto surrendered their registrations u/s 12AA of the I-T Act while admitting that some of their assets were not in compliance with the provisions of Section 13(1)(d) of the Act.

So, now the contentions of these six Tata Trusts that with reference to shares of TCS and Tata Capital held by these Trusts, the provisions of Section 13(1)(d) of the I-T Act would not be applicable as these shares were received by the Trusts as corpus donations and no investments has been made by these Trusts and that the investment in preference shares of Tata Sons Ltd was with the permission of the jurisdictional Commissioner of Income-tax and the same were redeemed in May 2016, seems to be contradictory to the findings of CAG and the suo-motto surrender of the registration by these six trusts consequent to their own admission of making investments in prohibited modes, and as such, needs to be examined and verified based on the actual facts, and evidences on record.

"There is precious little that's charitable about the world of charity."- Richard Cohen

So...

"Do your little bit of good where you are; it's those little bits of good put together that overwhelm the world." – Desmond Tutu

The LEGAL TWIST:

However, even if the findings of facts confirm to the fact of making investments in the prohibited modes by these six trusts as per provisions of section 13(1)(d), even then the registration of these six trusts can be cancelled only after 1.10.2014 and not before that, in view of above discussed undisputed legal position of Law, concerning the applicability of section 12AA(4) of the I-T Act, only w.e.f. 1.10.2014 only.

Also, in view of the stated legal precedents, only the dividend income being earned by these six Tata Trusts on the prohibited modes of investments in shares of Tata Group concerns can be denied exemption and not the other income of these trusts provided that such other income fulfils the stipulated condition of application of atleast 85% of such income towards the charitable objectives of the trusts u/s 11 of the I-T Act. Interestingly such dividend income which can be denied exemption u/s 11, as per the application of section 13(1)(d) of the Act, in any case were fully exempt in earlier years and to the extent of Rs. 10 lakhs by the Finance Act 2016, u/s 10(34) read with section 115BBDA of the I-T Act. As per the media reports, these six Trusts have also not availed the benefit of exemption u/s 11 of the I-T Act since AY 2016-17 onwards, after voluntary surrender of their registrations.

Non-Applicability of the provisions of section 115TD of the I-T Act:

As has already been discussed above that in order to ensure that the benefit conferred over the years to a charitable trust by way of exemption of its income u/s 11, is not being misused, section 115TD has been inserted with effect from June 1, 2016.

So, it is duly evident that this section can be pressed into service only w.e.f. 1.6.2016 and not before.

In a very recent and very high-profile judicial pronouncement of the Hon'ble Delhi ITAT in the case of **"Young Indian vs. CIT(Exemption), New Delhi"** in ITA No. 7751/Del/2017 dated 15.11.2019, Citation: **[2019] 111 taxman.com 235 (Delhi-Trib.)**, it has been observed and held by the Hon'ble Tribunal that the registration of a charitable trust ought to be cancelled from the date of contravention of any of the mandated conditions of granting registration.

Thus, in the present case of these six Tata Trusts, the registration of these six Trusts ought to be cancelled from the date when the prohibited investments in shares in the Tata Group concerns were being made by these six trusts as per provisions of section 12AA(4) read with section 13(1)(d) of the I-T Act.

However, since the provisions of section 12AA(4) of the I-T Act are applicable only w.e.f. 1.10.2014, therefore the cancellation of these six Tata Trusts can be lawfully made operative and effective w.e.f. 1.10.2014.

Therefore, the cancellation of these six Tata Trusts w.e.f. 31.10.2019 and the consequential pressing of service of the provisions of section 115TD of the I-T Act, by the Revenue Authorities, may not muster the tests of well settled and established legal jurisprudence in this regard. So, the correct, lawful and proper appreciation and understanding of the applicable legal provisions and legal jurisprudence in this regards could have prevented the pandora box of unproductive litigations which are eminent and unavoidable now, after the passing of the registration cancellation orders of these six trusts and the pressing of huge income tax demand u/s 115TD of the I-T Act.

"Less regulation plus less taxation plus less litigation always equals more innovation and job creation." -- Marsha Blackburn

TAXALOGUE 9

Joint Development Agreements: Income Tax Perspective

Introduction:

Joint Development Agreement (JDA) means an agreement or arrangement between the landowner and the developer wherein the land owner contributes the land to the project and the developer undertakes the construction/development of the said land into a developed estate, at mutually agreeable terms and conditions. Depending on the facts and circumstances of the case, multiple variations of this structure can be seen in the real estate sector, with the broad contours of the arrangement remaining the same.

Joint Development Agreements (JDAs) are a very common feature in the real estate sector and are beneficial to both the landowners and the developers. The developers are not required to make huge investments for the outright purchase of the land and thereby blocking their working capitals and the landowners can reap the benefits of the expertise of the developer in obtaining higher considerations for a developed estate rather than just the bare piece of land.

In a JDA, the landowner usually gets the consideration from the developer for contributing his land to the project and the said consideration may be in monetary terms or in non-monetary terms.

Monetary Consideration includes specified share in the sale consideration of the project as and when the collections from the customers are received. Non-monetary consideration includes specified share in the built-up/developed estate.

Direct Tax Perspective:

The income arising to the developer under a JDA, in the form of sale consideration of his share in the developed estate is considered as his business income and is taxed as per the applicable provisions.

The income arising to the landowner arising on transfer of title of land under a JDA, either in the form of specified share in the sale consideration or in the form of specified share in the developed estate, is considered as capital gain in his hands.

The taxability of capital gains in the hands of the landowner, arising on transfer of title of land from the land owner to the developer in a JDA has always been a litigative issue.

Legal Position uptill AY 2017-18:

For JDAs entered into on or before 31.3.2017:

Determination of the Taxable Event/Date of Transfer of Land by the landowner to the developer

Capital Gains arise on "transfer" of a capital asset. As per *Section 2(47)(v)* of the Income Tax Act 1961, the expression "transfer" amongst other things includes:

*"any transaction involving the allowing of the possession of any immovable property to be taken or retained in part performance of a contract of the nature referred to in **section 53A** of the Transfer of Property Act, 1882 (4 of 1882)"*

The Revenue Authorities, relying upon the above definition of transfer, have always contended that the taxability of the capital gains in the hands of the landowner, arising on transfer of title of land from the land owner to the developer in a JDA, arises as soon as the JDA is signed and entered into between the landowner and the developer.

Contrary to this, the assesses (landowners) contend that in a JDA, any consideration, either monetary in the form of specified share in the sale consideration or non-monetary in the form of specified share in the built-up/developed estate, accrues to the landowner, only after the construction/development of the developed estate, which entails a time period of atleast 2-3 years, and as such in the absence of accrual of any income in the hands of the landowners, at the time of signing/execution of the JDA, the taxable event does not arise.

Determination of Taxable Value of Consideration:

Considering the Revenue Authorities' contention of triggering of the taxable event at the time of signing/execution of the JDA, the biggest question which arises for consideration is when the project is just on papers at the time of signing of JDA, with no real existence, what would be the taxable value of consideration in the hands of the landowner.

The Revenue Authorities contended that as per the provisions of section 50D, which reads as under:

"Where the consideration received or accruing as a result of the transfer of a capital asset by an assessee is not ascertainable or cannot be determined, then, for the purpose of computing income chargeable to tax as capital gains, the fair market value of the said asset on the date of transfer shall be deemed to be the full value of the consideration received or accruing as a result of such transfer."

the taxable value of consideration in the hands of the landowner would be the fair market value of the project including land on the date of execution of the JDA.

This led to even more confusion and uncertainty, considering the fact that the projects under JDA run for an average 2 to 3 years and that the prices of real estate are subject to fluctuation, how could one determine an apt fair market value on the date of execution of JDA?

This contentious issue, to some an extent was resolved and addressed by the Hon'ble Supreme Court in its landmark judgement in the case of *"CIT v. Balbir Singh Maini"* Civil Appeal No. 15619 of 2017.

The Hon'ble Apex Court in the said case have considered the issue as to whether giving of possession of land for purposes of development under an unregistered joint development agreement could be regarded as giving rise to capital gains, and after referring to the 2001 amendment to the Registration Act, 1908, have categorically held that an unregistered agreement was not covered by section 53A of the Transfer of Property Act, 1908.

Further, the Hon'ble Apex Court also considered whether the signing of the joint development agreement or giving of possession could be said to be a transaction, which had the effect of transferring or enabling the enjoyment of the immovable property, which could also give rise to capital gains. According to the Apex Court, the purpose of this provision was to bring those transactions within the tax net, where, though title of the property was not transferred in law, there was, in substance, a transfer of title in fact. On a reading of the joint development agreement, the Hon'ble Court noted that the owner had continued to be the owner of the property throughout the development of the property, and had at no stage sought to transfer rights similar to ownership to the developer. At the most, only possession was given under the agreement and that too, for the limited purpose of development. The Hon'ble Apex Court, therefore, held that this clause also did not apply to the transaction, and that there was no transfer giving rise to capital gains.

Therefore, the principal ratio which emerged out of the above judgement of the Hon'ble Apex Court is that part performance of such an unregistered agreement (JDA) by the landowner, by giving possession of the property for the limited purpose of development, would not amount to a transfer, and hence did not give rise to capital gains.

Legal Position since AY 2018-19:

For JDAs entered into on or after 01.04.2018:

The Finance Act 2017 has inserted a new section 45(5A) in the Income Tax Act, 1961, which reads as under:

45(5A). Notwithstanding anything contained in sub-section (1), where the capital gain arises to an assessee, being an individual or a Hindu undivided family, from the transfer of a capital asset, being land or building or both, under a specified agreement, the capital gains shall be chargeable to income-tax as income of the previous year in which the certificate of completion for the whole or part of the project is issued by the competent authority; and for the purposes of section 48, *the stamp duty value, on the date of issue of the said certificate, of his share, being land or building or both in the project, as increased by the consideration received in cash, if any, shall be deemed to be the full value of the consideration received or accruing as a result of the transfer of the capital asset :*

Provided *that the provisions of this sub-section shall not apply where the assessee transfers his share in the project on or before the date of issue of the said certificate of completion, and the capital gains shall be deemed to be the income of the previous year in which such transfer takes place and the provisions of this Act, other than the provisions of this sub-section, shall apply for the purpose of determination of full value of consideration received or accruing as a result of such transfer.*

Explanation. – *For the purposes of this sub-section, the expression –*

(i) "competent authority" means the authority empowered to approve the building plan by or under any law for the time being in force;

(ii) "specified agreement" means a registered agreement in which a person owning land or building or both, agrees to allow

another person to develop a real estate project on such land or building or both, in consideration of a share, being land or building or both in such project, whether with or without payment of part of the consideration in cash;

(iii) "stamp duty value" means the value adopted or assessed or assessable by any authority of the Government for the purpose of payment of stamp duty in respect of an immovable property being land or building or both.]

Determination of the Taxable Event

As per the newly inserted subsection (5A) in section 45 of the Act, the taxable event i.e. the transfer of title of land by the landowner (only in the cases of individuals and HUFs) to the developer under a JDA, arises on receipt of the certificate of completion for the whole or part of the project, issued by the competent authority, provided the landowner does not transfer his share in the project to any other person on or before the date of issue of said certificate of completion.

Determination of Taxable Value of Consideration:

The newly inserted subsection (5A) in section 45 of the Act, provides that the stamp duty value of land or building or both, of the landowner's share in the project/developed estate, on the date of issuing of certificate of completion by the competent authority, to the land owner, as increased by any monetary consideration received by the landowner, if any, shall be deemed to be the full value of the consideration received or accruing as a result of the transfer of the capital asset, u/s 48 of the Act.

Legislative intent for introduction of Sec. 45(5A)

The Memorandum explaining the provisions of Finance Bill, 2017 states as under with respect to the introduction of Sec. 45(5A):

"With a view to minimise the genuine hardship which the owner of land may face in paying capital gains tax in the year of transfer, it is proposed to insert a new sub-section (5A) in section 45 so as to provide that in case of an assessee being individual or Hindu undivided family, who enters into a specified agreement for development of a project, the capital gains shall be chargeable to income-tax as income of the previous year in which the certificate of completion for the whole or part of the project is issued by the competent authority."

The amendment thus seeks to minimise the genuine hardships that the land owner may face by taxing the capital gains in its hands for area-sharing arrangements under JDA, in the previous year in which the certificate of completion is issued and not in the year in which the JDA is entered into or the possession of the land is given to the developer pursuant thereto.

Unaddressed Issues in the said amendment in section 45 of the Act:

(i) It has not been made clear as to why the benefit of the said amendment has been restricted only to individuals and HUFs and has not been extended to other persons/assesses entering into JDAs who shall continue to bear the hardship of prepayment of taxes.

(ii) The amendment seeks to defer the tax payment from entering into the JDA till receipt of the completion certificate. However, time limit for claiming benefit of exemption from long term capital gain u/s 54 & 54F continues to reckon from date of transfer (which as per Revenue Authorities' contention is the date of entering into the JDA) and has not been extended until the date of issuance of completion certificate.

(iii) It has also not been made clear as to whether the benefit of indexation on cost/improvement, as per Explanation to section 48, would be available till the year in which completion certificate has been received or only till the year in which the JDA has been entered into.

(iv) The newly inserted section 45(5A) of the Act provides for the adoption of stamp duty value of the land or building or both, of the landowner's share in the project/developed estate, on the date of issuing of certificate of completion by the competent authority, to the land owner, as the deemed full value of the consideration received or accruing as a result of the transfer of the capital asset, u/s 48 of the Act, in line with the similar provisions u/s 50C of the Act. However, unlike section 50C wherein a provision has been made to refer the valuation of the land and building to a valuation officer if the assessee challenges the adoption of stamp duty value, no such provision for reference to the valuation officer has been made in section 45(5A) of the Act.

Conclusion:

The recent amendments in the legislative provisions concerning the taxability of the income arising in a Joint Development Agreement (JDA), by way of insertion of a new subsection (5A) in section 45 of the Income Tax Act w.e.f. AY 2018-19, is indeed a welcome and positive development and initiative aimed at removing the uncertainty and confusion regarding the determination of the taxable event in a JDA and the taxable value of the consideration u/s 48 of the Act, for the purpose of taxation of the resultant capital gains in the hands of the landowners, and thereby providing the much needed relief to owners of property/land, being individuals or HUFs, who enter into JDA agreements. However, in order to make it more effective and fruitful, it is indeed the need of the hour that the Legislature and the concerned enforcement agencies must take cognizance of the above-mentioned unaddressed issues and address the same in right and earnest perspective.

TAXALOGUE 10

Are Sections 50C/43CA/56(2) of Income Tax Act Resulting in Double Taxation & Contrary to Real Income Theory?

The Finance Act 2002 has introduced a new section 50C with effect from 1-4-2003, for the purpose of computation of capital gains in real estate transactions, in the hands of seller of such land and/or building. Under this section the sale consideration as declared by the seller of land and/or building is to be substituted by the stamp duty valuation rate/circle rate of such land and/or building, in cases where the declared sale consideration is less than the corresponding stamp duty valuation rate/circle rate, for the purpose of calculating capital gains under Section 48 of the Income-tax Act, 1961.

The Explanatory Memorandum to the Finance Bill, 2002 explained the rationale of introduction of the said section 50C in the Direct Tax Laws as under:

"Computation of Capital Gains in Real Estate Transactions

The Bill proposes to insert a new section 50C in the Income-tax Act to make a special provision for determining the full value of consideration in cases of transfer of immovable property.

It is proposed to provide that where the consideration declared to be received or accruing as a result of the transfer of land or building or both, is less than the value adopted or assessed by any authority of a State Government for the purpose of payment of stamp duty in respect of such transfer, the value so adopted or assessed shall be deemed to be the full value of the consideration, and capital gains shall be computed accordingly under section 48 of the Income-tax Act.

It is further proposed to provide that where the assessee claims that the value adopted or assessed for stamp duty purposes exceeds the fair market value of the property as on the date of transfer, and he has not disputed the value so adopted or assessed in any appeal or revision or reference before any authority or Court, the Assessing Officer may refer the valuation of the relevant asset to a Valuation Officer in accordance with section 55A of the Income-tax Act. If the fair market value determined by the Valuation Officer is less than the value adopted for stamp duty purposes, the Assessing Officer may take such fair market value to be the full value of consideration. However, if the fair market value determined by the Valuation Officer is more than the value adopted or assessed for stamp duty purposes, the Assessing Officer shall not adopt such fair market value and will take the full value of consideration to be the value adopted or assessed for stamp duty purposes.

It is also proposed to provide that if the value adopted or assessed for stamp duty purposes is revised in any appeal, revision or reference, the assessment made shall be amended to recompute the capital gains by taking the revised value as the full value of consideration.

These amendments will take effect from 1st April, 2003 and will, accordingly, apply in relation to the assessment year 2003-2004 and subsequent years."

Similarly a new section 43CA has been incorporated in the Income Tax Act by the Finance Act, 2013. Under this section the sale consideration as declared by the seller of land and/or building is to be substituted by the stamp duty valuation rates/circle rates of such land and/or building, in cases where the declared sale consideration is less than the corresponding stamp duty valuation rates/circle rates, for the purpose of calculating income in the hands of seller under the head "Profits & Gains of Business or Profession".

The Explanatory Memorandum to the Finance Bill, 2013 explaining the rationale of introduction of the said section 43CA in the Direct Tax Laws provided as under:

"Computation of income under the head "profits and Gains of Business or Profession" for transfer of immovable property in certain cases

Currently, when a capital asset, being immovable property, is transferred for a consideration which is less than the value adopted, assessed or assessable by any authority of a State Government for the purpose of payment of stamp duty in respect of such transfer, then such value (stamp duty value) is taken as full value of consideration under section 50C of the Income-tax Act. These provisions do not apply to transfer of immovable property, held by the transferor as stock-in-trade.

It is proposed to provide by inserting a new section 43CA that where the consideration for the transfer of an asset (other than capital asset), being land or building or both, is less than the stamp duty value, the value so adopted or assessed or assessable shall be deemed to be the full value of the consideration for the purposes of computing income under the head "Profits and gains of business of profession".

It is also proposed to provide that where the date of an agreement fixing the value of consideration for the transfer of the asset and the date of registration of the transfer of the asset are not same, the stamp duty value may be taken as on the date of the agreement for transfer and not as on the date of registration for such transfer. However, this exception shall apply only in those cases where amount of consideration or a part thereof for the transfer has been received by any mode other than cash on or before the date of the agreement.

These amendments will take effect from 1st April, 2014 and will, accordingly, apply in relation to the assessment year 2014-15 and subsequent assessment years.

Since then, the Revenue Authorities are pressing into service the deeming fiction of substituting the declared sales consideration of land and/or building, by the stamp duty valuation rate/circle rate u/s 50C/43CA of the Act, and are re-computing the resultant capital gains/business gains respectively, on such deeming fiction basis, in the hands of the seller of such land and/or building.

Interestingly, the deeming fiction of taxability as envisaged in sections 50C and 43CA of the Income Tax Act, did not remain confined to just in the hands of seller of land and/or building and it has got extended in the hands of purchaser of land and/or building as well. There is one another section viz. 56(2)(*vii*)/56(2)(*x*) of the Income Tax Act, which provides for taxing the shortfall in the declared purchase consideration with that of the corresponding stamp duty valuation rate/circle rate of land and/or building in the hands of purchaser under the head 'income for other sources'.

Up till 1.4.2017, as per provisions of section 56(2)(*vii*), any sum of money or any property which was received without consideration or for inadequate consideration (in excess of the specified limit of Rs. 50,000) by an individual or HUF was chargeable to income-tax in the hands of the recipient under the head "Income from other sources". The definition of 'property' for the purpose of this section included immovable property, jewellery, shares, paintings, etc. The cases where the declared purchase consideration of land and/or building falls short of the corresponding stamp duty valuation rate/circle rate, were covered under the purview of the term 'inadequate consideration' in the context of receipt of an immovable property, by the purchaser.

The Finance Act, 2017 inserted a new clause (x) in sub-section (2) of section 56 so as to provide that receipt of the sum of money or the property by any person on or after 1-4-2017 without consideration or for inadequate consideration in excess of threshold limit of Rs. 50,000 shall be chargeable to tax in the hands of the recipient under the head "Income from other sources".

The Explanatory Memorandum to the Finance Bill, 2017 explained the rationale of the amendment as under:

"*Widening scope of Income from Other Sources*

Under the existing provisions of section 56(2)(vii), any sum of money or any property which is received without consideration or for inadequate consideration (in excess of the specified limit of Rs. 50,000) by an individual or HUF is chargeable to income-tax in the hands of the resident under the head "Income from other sources" subject to certain exceptions. Further, receipt of certain shares by a firm or a company in which the public are not substantially interested is also chargeable to income-tax in case such receipt is in excess of Rs. 50,000 and is received without consideration or for inadequate consideration. The existing definition of property for the purpose of this section includes immovable property, jewellery, shares, paintings, etc. These anti-abuse provisions are currently applicable only in case of individual or HUF and firm or company in certain cases. Therefore, receipt of sum of money or property without consideration or for inadequate consideration does not attract these anti-abuse provisions in cases of other assessees. In order to prevent the practice of receiving the sum of money or the property without consideration or for inadequate consideration, it is proposed to insert a new clause (x) in sub-section (2) of section 56 so as to provide that receipt of the sum of money or the property by any person without consideration or for inadequate consideration in excess of Rs. 50,000 shall be chargeable to tax in the hands of the recipient under the head "Income from other sources". It is also proposed to widen the scope of existing exceptions by including the receipt by certain trusts or institutions and receipt by way of certain transfers not regarded as transfer under section 47."

"Double Taxation"

In the existing framework of the Income Tax Act, for the same income or rather the deeming income, both the seller and the buyer of land and/or building, are being taxed twice and as such the pressing of service of such deeming fiction of taxation both in the hands of the seller and/or buyer of land and/or building is resulting in "Double Taxation". This 'double taxation' is contrary to the well-established and well settled principle of Law and canons of direct taxation that "a same income can't be taxed twice."

Time and again, numerous judgments of the Hon'ble Supreme Court and the Hon'ble High Courts have held the incidence and levy of 'double taxation' as unlawful and a nullity in the eyes of Law, prominent among these being the judgments of Hon'ble Supreme Court in the undermentioned cases viz.

(i) *Laxmipat Singhania* v. *CIT* **[1969] 72 ITR 291 (SC)**
(ii) *CIT* v. *Devi Prasad Vishwanath* **[1969] 72 ITR 194 (SC)**

The Legislature while preparing and legislating the Direct Taxation Laws has always kept in mind the unlawfulness and impermissibility of 'double taxation' of any particular income. The Income Tax Act contains numerous sections wherein the 'double taxation' of any income has been considered as impermissible and unlawful in the Act itself. The prominent examples include non-taxability of the partners' share of profits in the partnership firm/LLP, in the hands of partners by virtue of express exemption u/s. 10(2) of the Income Tax Act, non-taxability of Dividend income upto Rs. 10 lakhs, in the hands of recipient u/s. 115BBDA, the express provisions as contained in sections 90 and 91 of the Income Tax Act and the Double Taxation Avoidance

Agreements (DTAA) ensuring the avoidance of double taxation of income in two countries.

No doubt, the Constitution of India does not curtails or prohibits the Legislature for enacting and incorporating the express and specific provisions in the Income Tax Act resulting in 'double taxation', as has been presently done in incorporating section 56(2)(*vii*)/56(2)(*x*) in the Act, in addition to the prevailing section 50C/43CA of the Income Tax Act.

However, it is also desirable to keep in mind that such imposition of 'double taxation' even by express provisions in the Act is principally and fundamentally contrary to the principles of natural justice, equity and fair play and as such must be avoided by the Legislature. Just as any particular expenditure is allowable as tax deductible expenditure only in the hands of one particular assessee only and it is not allowed in the hands of two or more assessees, similarly the same income can't be taxed twice in the hands of one or more assessees.

Contrary to "Real Income Theory"

Further, this deeming fiction of taxation as envisaged in sections 50C, 43CA and 56(2)(x) of the Income Tax Act, needs to be examined from another perspective also, that is the "real income theory" perspective.

Time and again, numerous judgments of the Hon'ble Supreme Court and the Hon'ble High Courts have upheld the "real income theory" postulating the taxation of only real and actual income and not notional income.

Some of the significant judgments of Hon'ble Supreme Court in this regard are enumerated as under *viz.*

(*i*) *CIT v. Shoorji Vallabhdas & Co.* [1962] 46 ITR 144 (SC)

(*ii*) *CIT v. Chamanlal Mangaldas & Co.* [1960] 39 ITR 8 (SC)

(*iii*) *CIT v. Virtual Soft Systems Ltd.* [2018] 92 taxmann.com 370/255 Taxman 352/404 ITR 409 (SC)

(*iv*) *CIT v. Bokaro Steel Ltd.* [1999] 102 Taxman 94/236 ITR 315 (SC)

In view of the currently prevailing sluggishness and slow-down in the real estate sector, the property transactions of sale and purchase of land and/or building, in majority regions and areas, are taking place at prices/rates much below their respective circle/stamp duty valuation rates.

In such cases, the application of the provisions of section 50C/43CA/56(2), deeming the sale/purchase consideration equivalent to the applicable stamp duty/circle rates irrespective of the fact that the actual sale/purchase consideration is lesser than the circle rate, is resulting in a lot of undue hardships both in the hands of sellers as well as buyers, in the form of unwarranted and unjustified income tax liability on notional sale/purchase consideration towards immovable property.

It needs to be appreciated that the legislative intent of introduction of the said sections 50C/43CA/56(2) was to plug the cash dealings and under-recording and reporting of sale/purchase consideration of immovable properties in the arena, wherein market rates of immovable properties were substantially higher than their corresponding circle rates.

However, presently times have changed. Circle Rates have been revised on a substantially higher side whereas the market rates of immovable properties have comparatively fallen in view of the sluggishness in the real estate sector, and as such the gap between the market rates and circle rates of immovable properties has narrowed down considerably and infact in large number of areas and regions, the actual transaction rates/market rates of immovable properties are even lower than the circle rates.

The well-established and well settled "real income theory" postulates that only real and actual income can be taxed and any notional income can't be brought under the purview of taxation. However, the existing legal provisions as contained in sections 50C, 43CA and 56(2)(x) of the Income Tax Act, provides for the deeming fiction of taxing the notional income in those cases of sale and/or purchase of land and/or building, where the actual transaction rates/market rates of such immovable properties are even lower than the circle rates.

The provision for reference to valuation officer u/s. 55A of the Act, in cases where the assessee objects to the adoption of stamp duty valuation rate/circle rate in deeming the sale/purchase consideration, is also practically turning out to be a redundant and ineffective provision in view of the subjectivity and complexity involved in such valuation.

Concluding remarks:

In view of the changed dynamics of the demand & supply conditions in the real estate sector, there is an immediate and crucial need for the review, reconsideration and rationalisation of the existing provisions of section 50C/43CA/56(2)(x) of the Income Tax Act, providing for the unjustified adoption of stamp duty valuation rates/circle rates in deeming the sale/purchase consideration of immovable properties, even in those cases where the actual transaction rates/market rates are lower than the circle rates, so as to bring them in alignment with the actual transaction rates of immovable properties, in order to ensure the avoidance of "double taxation" both in the hands of sellers and buyers as well as to avoid the "taxation of notional income" contrary to the "real income theory" in order to provide the "ease of living" to the general masses and to provide the much needed push and fillip to the real estate sector.

TAXALOGUE 11

Applicability of Section 56(2) on Fresh /Bonus/Right Issue & Buy Back of Shares: An Undying Conundrum!!

The provisions of section 56(2)(viia) of the Income Tax Act were inserted w.e.f. the Finance Act 2010, and read as under:

> Section 56(2) : *"In particular, and without prejudice to the generality of the provisions of sub-section (1), the following incomes, shall be chargeable to income-tax under the head "Income from other sources", namely : –*
>
> *(viia) where a firm or a company not being a company in which the public are substantially interested, receives, in any previous year, from any person or persons, on or after the 1st day of June, 2010 [but before the 1st day of April, 2017], any property, being shares of a company not being a company in which the public are substantially interested, –*
>
> (i)   *without consideration, the aggregate fair market value of which exceeds fifty thousand rupees, the whole of the aggregate fair market value of such property;*

(ii) *for a consideration which is less than the aggregate fair market value of the property by an amount exceeding fifty thousand rupees, the aggregate fair market value of such property as exceeds such consideration:*

Provided that this clause shall not apply to any such property received by way of a transaction not regarded as transfer under clause (via) or clause (vic) or clause (vicb) or clause (vid) or clause (vii) of section 47.

Explanation. – For the purposes of this clause, "fair market value" of a property, being shares of a company not being a company in which the public are substantially interested, shall have the meaning assigned to it in the Explanation to clause (vii).

The provisions of above section 56(2)(viia) are applicable uptill 1.4.2017 and w.e.f. 1.4.2017 a new similar section 56(2)(x) has been inserted, which reads as under:

"(x) where any person receives, in any previous year, from any person or persons on or after the 1st day of April, 2017, –

(c) any property, other than immovable property, –

(A) without consideration, the aggregate fair market value of which exceeds fifty thousand rupees, the whole of the aggregate fair market value of such property;

(B) for a consideration which is less than the aggregate fair market value of the property by an amount exceeding fifty thousand rupees, the aggregate fair market value of such property as exceeds such consideration".

At present, the Revenue Authorities are pressing into service the above section 56(2)(viia) {applicable uptill 1.4.2017} and section 56(2)(x) {applicable from 1.4.2017}, to all kinds of receipts of shares by the specified company or firm as a result of subsequent transfer of unlisted shares as well as fresh issuance of shares including by way of bonus shares, rights shares and preference shares or transactions of similar nature.

The Central Board of Direct Taxes had issued Circular No. 10/2018 dated 31.12.2018 to clarify that provisions of section 56(2)(viia) of the Income-tax Act, 1961 being anti-abuse provisions shall not be applicable in cases of receipt of shares by the specified company or firm as a result of fresh issuance of shares including by way of bonus shares, rights shares and preference shares or transactions of similar nature by the specified company.

However, on reconsideration it was observed by CBDT that the matter relating to interpretation of the term 'receives' used in section 56(2)(viia) of the act is pending before judicial forums and stakeholders have sought clarifications on other similar provisions in section 56 of the Act. Accordingly, with the idea of issuing a fresh comprehensive circular on the subject, the circular no.10/2018 was withdrawn by circular no. 02/2019 dated 04.01.2019. While withdrawing the circular no. 10/2018, it was also clarified that the said circular shall be considered to have never been issued.

Subsequently, it was clarified by CBDT vide its circular no. 3/2019 dated 21.01.2019 that the view, taken in circular no. 10/2018 (subsequently withdrawn by circular no. 02/2019) that section 56(2)(viia) of the Act would not apply to fresh issuance of shares, would not be a correct approach, as it could be subject to abuse and would be contrary to the express provisions and the legislative intent of section 56(2)(viia) or similar provisions contained in section 56(2) of the Act. Accordingly, it was further clarified that any view expressed by the Board in Circular No. 10/2018 shall be considered to have never been expressed and, the said circular shall not be taken into account by any Income-tax authority in any proceedings under the Act.

Author's Humble Understanding & View on Above:

The Hon'ble CBDT has withdrawn its Circular No. 10/2018 dated 31.12.2018 concerning the non-applicability of provisions of section 56(2)(viia) of the Income Tax Act, in cases of receipt of shares by the specified company or firm as a result of fresh issuance of shares including by way of bonus shares, rights shares and preference shares or transactions of similar nature, by reasoning that it was contrary to the legislative intent.

However, **Ironically**, the view expressed in the said CBDT Circular No. 10/2018 dated 31.12.2018, suggesting the non-applicability of provisions of section 56(2)(viia) of the Income Tax Act, in cases of receipt of shares by the specified company or firm as a result of fresh issuance of shares including by way of bonus shares, rights shares and preference shares or transactions of similar nature, **was actually in complete harmony and conformity with the legislative intent of introduction of the said anti-abuse provision of section 56(2)(viia) by the Finance Act 2010.**

The **Explanatory Memorandum to Finance Bill 2010** explaining the rationale of introduction of the said section 56(2)(viia), interalia provided that,

> *"In order to prevent the practice of transferring unlisted shares at prices much below their market value, it is proposed to amend Section 56(2) to also include within its ambit, transactions undertaken in shares of a company (not being a company in which public are substantially interested) either for inadequate consideration or without consideration where recipient is a Firm or a Company"*

Thus it is amply clear and duly evident from above that the legislative intent of introduction of section 56(2)(viia) was to prevent the practice of transferring of unlisted shares at prices below their fair market value. The expression "transfer" has altogether different connotation and meaning than the expression "issuance" and as such the provisions of said section 56(2)(viia) were meant to be applicable in cases of receipt of shares by a company or a firm on subsequent transfer of unlisted shares after their initial issuance by the issuing company.

Concluding Remarks: Therefore, in view of the above stated legislative intent of introduction of section 56(2)(viia) of the Act and in order to give the much needed flexibility to the corporate sector in raising its capital for its genuine financial needs, a suitable amendment either by way of insertion of an explanation or a proviso in section 56(2)(viia) applicable uptill 1.4.2017 and section 56(2)(x) (applicable from 1.4.2017) of the Act to the effect that provisions of the said section are applicable only in cases of receipt of shares as a result of transfer of such shares and are not to be made applicable in cases of receipt of shares by the specified company or firm as a result of fresh issuance of shares including by way of bonus shares, rights shares and preference shares or transactions of similar nature, is desirable and should be considered by the Finance Ministry and CBDT in right earnest.

TAXALOGUE 12

Have Conventional Coercive Tax Recovery Measures Outlived their Utility?

As per the existing Legislative framework of the Direct Taxation Laws in our Country, the tax collection measures can broadly be classified into Pre-Assessment tax collection measures and Post Assessment tax collection measures.

The pre-assessment tax collection measures include tax collections by way of TDS, Advance Tax, and Self-Assessment Tax as per Chapter XVII of the Income Tax Act, 1961.

The post-assessment tax collection measures include collection of taxes by way of regular assessment taxes by way of conducting regular assessments u/s 143(3), exparte assessments u/s 144, income escaping assessments u/s 147 and the block assessments u/s 153A/153C pursuant to surveys u/s 133 or searches and seizures u/s 132 of the Income Tax Act, 1961.

The Legislature has casted the statutory onus and responsibility of compliance of the pre-assessment tax collection measures of payment of TDS, Advance Tax and Self-Assessment Tax on the assessees themselves. No doubt there are well defined and well laid out penal provisions including prosecution in the Income Tax Act which act as an effective deterrent for the non-tax paying and non-complying assessees but still by and large these pre-assessment tax collection measures are looked after well by the assessees themselves and the Income Tax Department's Machinery plays only a monitoring and regulatory role in such measures.

The Income Tax Department's Machinery comes into active play in the post-assessment tax collection measures including collection of regular assessment taxes arising out of conducting of regular assessments u/s 143(3), exparte assessments u/s 144, income escaping assessments u/s 147 and the block assessments u/s 153A/153C pursuant to surveys u/s 133 or searches and seizures u/s 132 of the Income Tax Act, 1961, by the Revenue Officials. The launching of prosecution proceedings u/s 276B also forms an integral part of such post-assessment tax collection measures.

Now after having such well-defined categorization, it would be interesting to know as to what is the respective contribution of the pre-assessment tax collection measures and the post-assessment tax collection measures in the total annual tax collection figures.

The gross annual Income Tax collections for the FY 2017-18 as per the latest available data of CAG Reports were Rs. 11.54 lakh crores. The pre-assessment tax collection measures in the form of TDS, Advance Tax and Self-Assessment Tax amounting to Rs. 9.76 lakh crores constituted approximately 85% of the gross income tax collections, and the post assessment tax collections of Rs. 98,975 crores by way of different Tax Assessments constituted only 8.57% of the gross income tax collections. These statistical figures speak for themselves.

Interestingly, for contributing towards this substantial share of 85% of the gross income tax collections by way of pre-assessment tax collection measures of TDS, Advance Tax and Self-Assessment Tax, the assessees do not get rewarded in any manner. Infact to the contrary, a failure or default in discharge of this burden, even an unintentional one, results in some very dire consequences including prosecution also.

The Hon'ble Finance Minister Smt. Nirmala Sitharaman, while presenting the Union Budget 2019-20, before the Parliament, in her maiden budget speech in Modi 2.0 Government, has commenced with her Direct Tax Proposals by thanking and acknowledging the valuable contribution of taxpayers in the all-round growth of our Nation.

At this juncture, she found wisdom in a line from Pura Nanooru, a Tamil Sangam Era work by Pisirandaiyaar. The verse ," Yannai pugundha nilam" was sung as an advice to the King Pandian Arivudai Nambi, the English translation of which comes out as under:

"a few mounds of rice from paddy that is harvested from a small piece of land would suffice for an elephant. But what if the elephant itself enters the field and starts eating? What it eats would be far lesser than what it would trample over!"

Admiringly, in the above verse, by referring the Government as the Elephant, the Taxpayer as the Farmer of the Paddy Field and the Mounds of Rice as the Income-tax Collections, the importance, significance and effectiveness of tax rationalisation measures aimed at ensuring voluntary compliance and tax deposition by taxpayers as against the coercive tax recovery measures, has been emphasised and encouraged by the Hon'ble Finance Minister.

The regulatory body CBDT has also, always emphasized on creating and providing a taxpayer friendly regime.

However, this intent and thought process of the Law making and regulatory authorities in encouraging and rewarding voluntary compliance by taxpayers and ensuring the 'taxpayer friendly regime' should not merely be on paper and it should infact be reflected in the actual conduct of the law enforcing agencies and the Revenue Authorities, while conducting tax assessments and collecting taxes from the assessees.

The logo of the Income Tax Department "कोष मूलो दण्ड:" as adopted from the *'Kautilya's Arthashastra'* actually means "Revenue is the backbone of Administration."

However, going by the present day tendency of the Revenue Authorities to put undue pressure on the assessees for tax collections for meeting out budgetary targets for improving service records by using the window of survey, search & seizure and even prosecution, it appears that the logo "कोष मूलो दण्ड:" has been interpreted by the tax collecting authorities as to mean that *'in the core of revenue collection, lies the punishment.'*

In the regular assessments u/s 143(3), the making of huge additions/disallowances even on unlawful and factually misconceived grounds and raising of huge income tax demands have become a regular and common phenomenon. In such high-pitched assessments, the assessee is being compelled to deposit atleast 20% of such high-pitched demands and any failure on the part of the assessee even a non-intentional one, results in seizure of his bank accounts and even in taking recourse to the extreme coercive tax recovery measures of attachment of properties and prosecution.

The sacrosanct window of income escaping assessment u/s 147 of the Act is being used as a habitual and casual opportunity of reopening the already concluded assessments any number of times within the maximum stipulated period of six years, and thereby demeaning and disregarding the very sanctity and conclusivity of the completed assessments.

Such additions/disallowances made on merits and duly corroborated and substantiated by corresponding material and evidences and not just conjectures, surmises and presumptions and such re-openings of already concluded assessments based on tangible, reliable, material and concrete basis of reason to believe are always welcome and appreciable, and the concerned revenue officials should be applauded and duly rewarded for bringing to fore the habitual and willful tax defaulters.

However, making of huge additions/disallowances in assessments, just for the sake of making additions and reopening the already concluded assessments u/s 147, just for the sake of re-opening and creating hefty fictitious income tax demands and completely ignoring the well settled and established binding legal precedents even of the Hon'ble Supreme Court, being contrary to the very intent of the Legislature, must be avoided and infact effective deterrent provisions in the scheme of the Act itself must be incorporated to fix the accountability and responsibility of the errant revenue officials.

Similarly, in the survey u/s 133 and search & seizure action u/s 132 of the Act, the high-handed approach and the coercive tax recovery measures are integrally prevalent in the tax administration system. Entire focus is being put on forcing admissions by the assessees of the concealment of income and tax evasion by resorting to undue pressure tactics. This is followed by making of huge additions/disallowances in the block assessments u/s 153A/153C, and thereby raising huge income tax demands on the assessees.

And in doing so, the well-established and well settled position of Law stipulating the mandatory requirement of unearthing of the incriminating material and evidences during the course of such surveys and searches, in substantiation and corroboration of the alleged concealment of income or tax evasion, as per numerous binding judgements of Hon'ble High Courts and even the Hon'ble Supreme Court, is very conveniently ignored and disregarded and the assessee is again being compelled to battle out the vicious circle of depositing huge income tax demands and fighting litigations on various appellate forums.

In resorting to such coercive tax recovery measures, including seizure of bank accounts, conducting surveys and searches, attaching properties and launching prosecutions, even against the bonafide and circumstantial defaulters, the Tax Authorities somehow adopt a very short sighted approach and vision of meeting out their budgetary tax collection targets for a particular financial year and in the process they miss out on a much bigger picture and perspective concerning the future revenue generation and employment generation potential of such bonafide entrepreneurs and taxpayers, one such case in point being the recent unfortunate demise of the owner of *Café Coffee Day Sh. V.G. Siddhartha.*

Numerous researches based on sound empirical evidences and even the tax collection data and statistical figures of the Income Tax Department itself have made it duly evident and amply clear that the ultimate tax-realization out of such coercive tax recovery measures is almost nothing in comparison to the huge cost involved in undertaking such measures both in terms of money, manpower, time & resources as well as in terms of loss of goodwill and taxpayer friendly image of the law enforcing agencies and the Government.

Concluding Remarks:

In order to bring to fore the 'Ease of Doing Business' and the 'Taxpayer Friendly Regime' in reality and not just on papers, there is a serious and grave urgency of overhauling and rationalizing of the entire tax administration and the tax regulatory environment and eco-system so as to enable an effective, lucrative and merit-based tax-realisation from the willful and habitual tax defaulters and incentivisation of the honest and compliant tax payers, who create wealth for the Nation.

Ultimately, the tax administration authorities, must not forget their genesis and roots stemming from the ancient robust and well-defined tax administration systems outlined in the 'Kautilya's Arthashastra' and the Manu's

'Manu-Smriti', wherein it has been categorically advised that,

"यथाऽल्पाल्पमदन्त्याद्यं वार्योकोवत्सषट्पदाः।
तथाऽल्पाल्पो ग्रहीतव्यो राष्ट्राद् राज्ञाब्दिकः करः॥१२८(१२९)॥"

Meaning thereby that, "As the water-insect, the calf and the bee eat their food little by little, so little by little should the King draw from his kingdom the annual taxes. — (128)

And also,

"यथा फलेन युज्येत राजा कर्ता च कर्मणाम् ।
तथाऽवेक्ष्य नृपो राष्ट्रे कल्पयेत् सततं करान् ॥ १२९ (१२८) ॥

Meaning thereby that, "After due investigation the King shall always levy taxes in his kingdom in such a way that he himself and the man who carries on the business shall both receive their reward. — (129).

TAXALOGUE 13

Review of the Existing Prosecution Provision u/s 276B of the Income Tax Act, 1961- Need of the Hour is to Take Taxpayer Friendly Initiative.

Legislature, by the insertion of Chapter XVII-B in the Income Tax Act, 1961, has casted the responsibility of deducting and depositing Tax at Source (TDS) in relation to the income of the recipient, upon the payer of such income and as such the statutory onus and burden of the Exchequer has been shifted to the payer of income who happens to be an assessee. In the FY 2015-16, TDS constituted approximately 42 % of the nett. income tax collections and 36% of the gross income tax collections. Pre-Assessment Tax Collection Measures in the form of TDS, Advance Tax and Self-Assessment Tax constituted approximately 85% of the gross income tax collections of Rs 8.64 lakh crores. Interestingly, for discharging this statutory responsibility of the Exchequer, the assessee does not get rewarded in any manner. Infact to the contrary, a failure or default in discharge of this burden, even an unintentional one, results in some very dire consequences including prosecution also.

Section 276B of the Income Tax Act, 1961, providing for the prosecution provision in case of default in payment of TDS under Chapter XVII-B and Chapter XII-D, was inserted by the Finance Act, 1968, for the first time by the legislature.

The text of section 276B as inserted by the Finance Act, 1968 is reproduced as under:

"276B. If a person, without reasonable cause or excuse, fails to deduct or after deducting fails to pay the tax as required by or under the provisions of sub-section (9) of section 80E or Chapter XVII-B, he shall be punishable with rigorous imprisonment for a term which may extend to six months, and shall also be liable to fine which shall be not less than a sum calculated at the rate of fifteen per cent per annum on the amount of such tax from the date on which such tax was deductible to the date on which such tax is actually paid]."

The provisions of section 276B of the Income Tax Act, have undergone multiple changes since last 5 decades and presently this section as per Finance Act 2017, reads as under:

"276B. If a person fails to pay to the credit of the Central Government, the tax deducted at source by him as required by or under the provisions of Chapter XVII-B, he shall be punishable with rigorous imprisonment for a term which shall not be less than three months but which may extend to seven years and with fine."

The journey which this section 276B of the Income Tax Act, 1961 has transcended over the last 5 decades is clearly not in favour of the assessee and is not taxpayer friendly.

A perusal of the afore-stated legal position as enshrined u/s 276B, at two points of time i.e. at the time of its insertion in 1968 and at present in 2017, makes it abundantly clear that this provision has been made more stringent and harsher with the passage of time.

This is evident as under:
(i) the expression "without reasonable cause or excuse" which was very much an integral part of the section at the time of its insertion in 1968, and is in line with the cardinal principal of equity, justice and good conscience has altogether been omitted at present.
(ii) the maximum tenure of imprisonment has been increased from 6 months to 7 years.

However, there is a *non obstante* provision as contained in section 278AA of the Income Tax Act, 1961, which clearly provides that no person shall be punishable for any failure referred to in section 276B if he proves that there was a reasonable cause for such failure.

There is a well-known maxim which goes as *"with great power comes greater responsibility."* The Power to Prosecute must be used judiciously, rationally and with due application of mind to meet the ends of justice.

The prosecution for default in paying TDS to the credit of the Central Government did not automatically follow such default and the provision had, therefore, been made under section 279 of the Income-tax Act for sanction to be granted for such prosecution by the Chief Commissioner. It had repeatedly been held by the courts that whenever the decision was left to the subjective satisfaction of a statutory authority, it necessarily implied that such authority was required to apply its mind to all relevant factors before arriving at a decision. The grant of sanction for launching prosecution is a very serious & extreme measure having serious consequences which entailed proper exercise of discretion upon consideration of all relevant materials, including mitigating circumstances in favour of the defaulter.

However, unfortunately, the present-day tendency has become to put undue pressure for tax collections for meeting out budgetary targets for improving service records, by using the window of prosecution. This was clearly not the Legislative Intent behind insertion of Prosecution Provisions in the Income Tax Act, 1961.

Surprisingly and Shockingly, the Current Legal Provisions and the CBDT guidelines, w.r.t. section 276B of the Income Tax Act, concerning the default in payment of TDS in time, entails very serious and harsh consequences. Presently, there are numerous instances, where even for a delay of 2-3 months in depositing the TDS with the Exchequer, Prosecution Proceedings u/s 276B are being launched. This high-handed approach is clearly not justifiable and desirable.

The present framework of law in the context of section 276B of the Income Tax Act, treats every assessee who has defaulted in payment of TDS, on equal footing, irrespective of the severity of default. This is totally unwarranted and uncalled for.

For judicious, equitable and effective implementation of the Prosecution Provision u/s 276B of the Income Tax Act, first and foremost, the defaulters must be categorized into different categories based on the nature and severity of default in terms of quantum, duration and intent parameters and depending upon the severity of the default, the penal consequences must follow.

In making these categorizations, the element of subjectivity within the categorization must be altogether done away with. Instead the entire categorization exercise must be standardized as is being done in Computer Assisted Scrutiny Selection (CASS).

In determining the categorization of defaulters, the status of pendency or otherwise of the regular undisputed income- tax refund of the defaulter assessee deserves to be given a significant and major consideration.

This can be better explained in terms of 2 Hypothetical Scenarios as under:

Scenario 1. An assessee X, defaults in deposition of TDS amounting to Rs 20 Lacs, and even after the lapse of more than 12 months, he has not deposited the principal TDS amount as well as the penal interest. No income tax refund is pending in his PAN.

Scenario 2. An assessee Y, defaults in deposition of TDS amounting to Rs 20 Lacs. He deposits the principal TDS amount as well as the penal interest @ 1.5% per month after a delay of 6 months. However, his regular undisputed income-tax refund of more than Rs. 20 Lacs or much more than Rs. 20.00 Lacs is also pending with the Exchequer, and it remains pending through-out the period of default in payment of TDS by him and thereafter.

In this case, assessee X in scenario 1 is obviously a willful defaulter and appropriate penal actions against him are warranted.

However, the question arises in the case of assessee Y in scenario 2. Whether it will be justifiable or rational to consider assessee Y as an assessee in default u/s 201 and whether it is lawful to launch prosecution proceedings u/s 276B against him. Going by the true legislative intent and the dictum of principle of natural justice, the answer shall be "NO" only. This is because, in real and effective terms, at no point of time, there is outstanding income-tax demand against assessee Y. The TDS demand of assessee Y can very easily be adjusted against his pending regular income-tax refund and so assessee Y must not be considered as an assessee in default and the question of launching of prosecution proceedings against assessee Y must not arise, more so when he has paid the principal TDS along with the penal interest @ 1.5% per month, whereas he is entitled for a comparatively very less interest on his income-tax refund @ 0.5% per month only.

The afore-stated hypothetical scenario 2, ironically reflects the clearly evident lack of level playing field for the assessee. This is so because, if there is some default in payment of TDS in time by the assessee, he is liable to pay penal interest @ 1.5% per month and also suffers the disallowance of corresponding expenditure in computation of his taxable income. To add to that, he is also exposed to prosecution u/s 276B of the Income Tax Act and to avoid that the assessee is forced to apply for compounding wherein he is supposed to pay additional interest @ 3% per month along with the applicable compounding charges.

As opposed to this, if there is a delay in granting the income-tax refund by the Exchequer to the assessee, all he can hope for is a compensating interest @ 0.5% per month and that too after a lot of follow-up and litigation. There is no provision in Law for compounding against the Exchequer. No prosecution can be launched against the Exchequer and unlike the assessee, the Exchequer can't be considered as an Exchequer in default.

There are cases, where the outstanding income-tax refund of the assessee is 3-4 times as that of his TDS liability. In such cases, the delay in granting the due income tax refund to the assessee impacts the business & the financial capability of the assessee very severely & adversely & also results in the credit facilities of the assessee becoming NPAs much to the detriment of the Exchequer as well as the assessee. In such cases, it would not be wrong to contend that the assessee's inability to deposit the TDS in time, is primarily because the Exchequer has not provided his due income tax refund. In such cases, even if the Exchequer launches prosecution, it is not likely to sustain in the Court of Law & rather it will be difficult for the Exchequer to defend its own delay in granting refund of income tax to the assessee.

In order to restore some balance, atleast in cases where there is default in payment of TDS but simultaneously the regular income-tax refund is also pending in the name of the assessee, then the assessee must be given an option to get its outstanding TDS demand adjusted against its pending income tax refund and this will enable the recipient of income also to obtain his TDS credit in time. Currently, even after penalizing the deductor for his default in deposition of TDS by way of levy of penal interest @ 1.5% per month and disallowance of the corresponding expenditure and further more by subjecting him to compounding @ 3% per month in lieu of launching prosecution proceedings u/s 276B, no credit of TDS is being made available to the recipient of income. Thus, in true spirit, the whole purpose of subjecting the deductor to all these stringent repercussions gets defeated.

Furthermore, the online Form 26AS in which the credit of TDS being deducted from the income of the recipient, is reflected, instead of serving as a taxpayer friendly initiative, is infact causing undue hardship to the recipient of income. This is because, currently there are numerous instances where due to the inherent processing deficiencies in this online system, the TDS credit does not get reflected even after the same has been deposited by the deductor and the deductee gets deprived of his lawful TDS credit. Unfortunately, currently the non-reflection of even the duly deducted and deposited TDS in online Form 26AS, is being used as a blanket excuse for not giving the fully lawful TDS credit. Before the induction of this online system, based on the manual TDS certificates, the deductee was atleast able to claim his otherwise lawful TDS credit. The vigour, aggressiveness and willingness as shown by the Exchequer in penalizing the Tax Deductor must also be reflected in giving hindrance free TDS credit to the deductee.

All what is required is a proper co-ordination between the TDS Wing and the Assessment Wing of the Exchequer and the removal of the procedural bottlenecks and streamlining of the functional capacities of the Exchequer. Currently u/s 245 of the Income Tax Act, the outstanding income tax demand of the assessee is being adjusted against his income tax refund. The same must also apply to the adjustment of the pending TDS demand as reflected in Traces against income tax refund. This will lead to the much-needed avoidance of undue hardship to both the payer of income and recipient of income. Also, it will result in substantial reduction in the administrative work-load of the Exchequer and will enable it to direct its time and energy in harnessing tax revenues in a more efficient and productive manner.

An assessee who has deposited the deducted TDS with penal interest and has filed the TDS Returns, must not be considered as a defaulter anymore. He can't be equated with a Tax Evader. Thousands of such prosecution notices are being sent by the Exchequer to the Business Community across the country w.e.f. FY 12-13. There are thousands of cases, wherein the harassment of Law abiding assessees, becomes clearly evident. Even the Exchequer is also being burdened un-necessarily.

Therefore, keeping in view the above, the concerned Revenue Authorities must review this existing stringent provision u/s 276B of the Income Tax Act and must consider doing appropriate modifications/changes in it so as to enable an effective action against the willful and habitual tax evaders only and not against the bonafide assessees who create wealth for the Nation. Then in true spirit, the Government's Objective of enabling and facilitating Ease of Doing Business will be accomplished.

TAXALOGUE 14

TDS on Power Transmission & Wheeling Charges u/s 194I/194J & 194C of Income Tax Act

Has the Contentious Issue of Applicability or Otherwise of TDS on Transmission & Wheeling Charges of Power Transmission Companies u/s 194J, 194I & 194C of the Income Tax Act, 1961, finally Settled?

The activity of distribution of electricity by power distribution companies, to end consumers, is preceded by two important intermediate steps – namely production of electricity by power generation companies and its transmission from point of production to the point of distribution, by power transmission companies.

The process of transmission of electricity from the generation point of the power generation company to the distribution point of the power distribution company through the transmission system network of the transmission company, in technical parlance is termed as "Wheeling".

For availing the benefits of this standard facility viz. the transmission system network of power transmission companies, for the purpose of transmission of electricity from the generation point to the distribution point, the power distribution companies make payment of the

Transmission & Wheeling Charges to the transmission companies. The Transmission & Wheeling Charges are determined by concerned State Electricity Regulatory Commissions, which are Regulatory Bodies constituted under the Electricity Regulatory Commission Act.

The issue of applicability or otherwise of TDS on transmission and wheeling charges, has always been a contentious and litigative issue. The Revenue Authorities, have, time and again, subjected the said transmission & wheeling charges, to the deduction of TDS, by the power distribution companies, either under section 194J, or u/s 194I or u/s 194C. Interestingly, this hit and trial approach, makes it amply clear that even Revenue Authorities themselves, are not very clear about the exact nature of the transmission & wheeling charges, so as to apply a standard section for the purpose of TDS deductibility.

It will be worthwhile to examine the applicability or otherwise of TDS on Transmission & Wheeling Charges, under all the stated three sections viz. section 194J, 194I & 194C of the Income Tax Act, as under:

(I) APPLICABILITY OR OTHERWISE OF TDS ON TRANSMISSION & WHEELING CHARGES U/S 194J OF THE INCOME TAX ACT:

The Revenue Authorities, very often, consider "Transmission & Wheeling Charges", as "Fees for Technical Services", u/s 194J of the Act.

Explanation to section 194J, defines "technical services", as:

(b) "fees for technical services" shall have the same meaning as in Expln. 2 to cl. (vii) of sub-s. (1) of s. 9;"

Explanation 2 to Sec. 9(1)(vii) of the Act provides that, "For the purposes of this clause, "fees for technical services" means any consideration (including any lump sum consideration) for the rendering of any managerial, technical or consultancy services (including the provision of services of technical or other personnel) but does not include consideration for any construction, assembly, mining or like project undertaken by the recipient or consideration which would be income of the recipient chargeable under the head "Salaries."

However, there is a need to appreciate & recognize the distinction between "Technical Services" & "Technology Driven Services".

Technical Service referred to in Explanation 2 to section 9(1)(vii) of the Act contemplates rendering of a technical service to the payer of the fees & not technology driven services.

Installation & operation of sophisticated equipments with a view to earn income by allowing the users to avail the benefits of such equipments does not tantamount to rendering of "Technical Services" within the meaning of Explanation 2 to section 9(1)(vii) of the Act.

Mere collection of a fee for making available a standard facility provided to all those willing to pay for it does not amount to the fees having been received for technical services.

Where a person has developed a technical system consisting of sophisticated instruments and the technical ability and knowledge to operate and maintain the system, it does not result in providing any technical service to others. Rendering of services by using some sophisticated equipments/ technical systems is different from charging fees for rendering technical services.

The power distribution companies make payment of transmission & wheeling charges to the transmission companies, in consideration of availing the benefits of the standard technical facility viz. the Transmission System Network of the transmission companies, for the purpose of transmission of electricity from the generation point to the distribution point and as such by merely making available the benefits of its sophisticated Transmission System Network to the distribution company, the transmission company does not render any "Technical Services" within the meaning of Explanation 2 to section 9(1)(vii) of the Act. Also, the benefits of the said standard facility viz. the transmission system network of "RVPN" may be availed by any distribution company within the framework & guidelines of prescribed open access transmission norms.

The Hon'ble Delhi High Court in the case of "CIT vs. Bharati Cellular Limited [175 Taxmann 573 (Del)]", has categorically held that technical services which are relevant for the purpose of section 194J would be those technical services which involve human interface/element. In other words, the expression 'technical service' could have reference to only technical service rendered by a human and that it would not include my service provided by machines or robots.

The said judgment of the Hon'ble Delhi High Court, has been affirmed by the Hon'ble Supreme Court in 193 Taxman 97(SC).

Without prejudice to above analysis, this aspect can be looked at, from another perspective also.

The respective State Governments, confer the status of "State Transmission Utility (STU), to the concerned power transmission companies.

Sec. 39 of the Electricity Act, 2003 mandates the STU to undertake various functions wherein sub-s. (2) of s. 39 provides as under ;

"(2) The functions of the STU shall be –

(a) to undertake transmission of electricity through intra-state transmission system;

(b) to discharge all functions of planning and co-ordination relating to intra-state transmission system with —

(i) Central transmission utility;

(ii) State Governments;

(iii) Generating companies;

(iv) Regional power committees;

(v) Authority;

(vi) Licensees;

(vii) any other person notified by the State Government in this behalf;

(c) to ensure development of an efficient, co-ordinated and economical system of intra-State transmission lines for smooth flow of electricity from a generating station to the load centers;

(d) to provide non-discriminatory open access to its transmission system for use by —

(i) any licensee or generating company on payment of the transmission charges; or

(ii) any consumer as and when such open access is provided by the State Commission under sub-s. (2) of s. 42, on payment of

the transmission charges and a surcharge thereon, as may be specified by the State Commission" :

Further, Sec. 34 provides that every transmission licensee shall comply with such technical standards of operation and maintenance of transmission lines, in accordance with grid standards as may be specified by authority. These grid standards are described in Indian electricity code prescribed by Central Electricity Regulatory Commission.

From the aforestated provisions of the Electricity Act, 2003, it becomes clear that all the entities involved in generation, transmission and distribution of electricity are discharging their respective statutory functions and are complying with the directions of State Load Dispatch Centre and the Regulatory Commission for achieving the economy and efficiency in the operation of power system and therefore question of any entity rendering any technical service to another does not arise.

The aforesaid views also get fortified by the decision of the Hon'ble Delhi High Court in the case of CIT vs. Delhi Transco Ltd. (62 taxmann.com 166) (Del) (2015), wherein the Hon'ble Delhi High Court vide para no. 34 & 35, has held as under:-

"34. To reiterate, by virtue of the BPTA agreement between DTL and PGCIL there is transportation of the electricity from PGCIL to DTL, through the equipment and network required

statutorily to be maintained by PGCIL through its technical personnel using technical expertise. This, however, does not result in PGCIL providing technical services to DTL. Therefore the wheeling charges paid by DTL and PGCIL for such transportation of electricity cannot be characterized as fee for technical service.

35. The ultimate conclusion of the ITAT is therefore not erroneous. Accordingly the question framed by the Court is answered in the negative i.e., against the Revenue and in favour of the Assessee. Since the same question is involved in all the AYs in question, all these appeals are dismissed affirming the impugned order of the ITAT, but in the circumstances with no order as to costs."

Against the aforesaid decision of the Hon'ble Delhi High Court in the case of CIT vs. Delhi Transco Limited (Supra), the Revenue Authorities, went in Appeal before the Hon'ble Supreme Court of India in SLP(C) No. 853/2016 in the case of CIT(TDS) vs. Delhi Transco Limited, which has since been dismissed by the Apex Court vide its order dated 22/01/2016 by holding as under:-

"We find no reason to entertain this Special Leave Petition, which is, accordingly dismissed."

Therefore, the present legal position, in relation to the applicability of TDS on Transmission & Wheeling Charges, u/s 194J of the Act, stands settled and concluded by the aforestated dismissal of Special Leave Petition (SLP), of Revenue Authorities, by the Hon'ble Apex Court in SLP(C) No. 853/2016 in the case of CIT (TDS) vs. Delhi Transco Limited, and as such the transmission & wheeling charges, can't be considered as "Fees for Technical Services" so as to attract TDS applicability u/s 194J of the Act.

(II) APPLICABILITY OR OTHERWISE OF TDS ON TRANSMISSION & WHEELING CHARGES U/S 194I OF THE INCOME TAX ACT:

The meaning of Rent as specifically provided by Explanation to section 194I of the Act is as follows:

Explanation to S. 194I: For the purposes of this section,-

"(i) "rent" means any payment, by whatever name called, under any lease, sublease, tenancy or any other agreement or arrangement for the use of (either separately or together) any,-

(a) land; or

(b) building (including factory building); or

(c) land appurtenant to a building (including factory building); or

(d) machinery; or

(e) plant; or

(f) equipment; or

(g) furniture; or

(h) fittings,

whether or not any or all of the above are owned by the payee."

It is clearly evident that the key words in this definition are *"for the use of"*. In other words, to consider any payment as rent u/s 194I, it must be towards the use of any particular asset.

The Revenue Authorities, contend that the transmission & wheeling charges, paid by distribution companies to transmission companies, are consideration towards the use of plant & machinery i.e. transmission system network of the transmission companies, and as such are liable for deduction of TDS u/s 194I of the Act.

However, this contention of the Revenue Authorities, ignores one basic fact that in order to use any plant & machinery or equipment, so as to come under the purview of TDS applicability u/s 194I of the Act, one has to have the physical possession or custody of the same. In other words one can't use anything which one does not possess.

The transmission system networks apart from being owned, managed, controlled & operated by the transmission companies, are always in the physical custody and possession of transmission companies only and not the distribution companies. Thus, the availment of the benefits of a standard facility i.e. transmission system network of the transmission companies, by the distribution companies, can't be considered as "use" of the same by the distribution companies, so as to attract TDS liability u/s 194I of the Act.

Reliance can be placed on the judgment of the Hon'ble Bombay High Court, in the case of "CIT vs. M/s Maharashtra State Electricity Distribution Company Ltd., in ITA No. 336 of 2013, dated 8.5.2015, wherein the Hon'ble Bombay High Court, has held that,

"36. The argument of the revenue that payments to MSETCL amounts to rent cannot be accepted. According to the Black's Law Dictionary, 'Rent' is defined as consideration paid for periodical use or occupancy of property. Various types of rent are contemplated such as ceiling rent, crop rent, ground rent, etc. Even taking the widest possible definition of rent, in our view the WT charges cannot be considered as rent. It is well settled that the Court may in its discretion construe the legislative provisions so as giving effect to the intended use and applying the test of contextual interpretation. We are of the view that the expression 'rent' used in Section 194-I does not apply to WT charges or any other part thereof.

37. In our view, the expression rent would also entail an element of possession. In each of the instances contemplated by the explanation to Section 194-I, we see in them an element of

possession, be it land, building (including factory building), land appertaining to a building, plant, equipment, furniture or fittings. The person using it has some degree of possessory control, at least momentarily, although it cannot entrust the user title to the subject matter of the charge. Even the mere right to "use" is vested with an element of possessory control over the subject matter. In the present case, WT charges are bereft of such possessory control and hence in our view, completely outside the purview of the Explanation to Section 194-I. "

Similar reliance can be placed upon the Judgement of the Honourable Authority For Advance Ruling in the case of "Dell International Services India (P) Ltd. (2008) 305 ITR 37.

The relevant extracts of the key observations & findings of the Hon'ble Authority in this regard are as follows:

"12.8. The word 'use' in relation to equipment occurring in (iv.a) is not to be understood in the broad sense of availing of the benefit of an equipment. The context and collocation of the two expressions 'use' and 'right to use' followed by the words "equipment" suggests that there must be some positive act of utilization, application or employment of equipment for the desired purpose.

If an advantage is taken from sophisticated equipment installed and provided by another, it is difficult to say that the recipient/customer uses the equipment as such. The customer merely makes use of the facility, though he does not himself use the equipment."

The Hon'ble ITAT Mumbai Bench, in the case of Chattisgarh State Electricity Board (CG State Power Holding Co. Ltd. vs ITO (TDS), 143 TTJ 151, has also categorically held that,

"17. ....When control of the asset (transmission lines in the present case) always remains with the PGCIL, any payment made to the PGCIL for transmission of power on the transmission lines and infrastructure owned controlled and in physical possession of PGCIL cant be said to have been made for the use of these transmission lines or other related infrastructure.

Viewed in this perspective, Section 194I has no application so far as the impugned payments for transmission of electricity is concerned."

Therefore, in view of aforesaid legal and factual propositions, transmission & wheeling charges, paid by the power distribution companies, for availing the benefits of transmission system networks of power transmission companies, can't be considered as rent for use of such network, so as to attract TDS applicability u/s 194I of the Act.

(III) APPLICABILITY OR OTHERWISE OF TDS ON TRANSMISSION & WHEELING CHARGES U/S 194C OF THE INCOME TAX ACT:

The Revenue Authorities contend that, if transmission & wheeling charges, can't be considered as either fees for technical services u/s 194J or rent u/s 194I of the Act, then alternatively, they may be considered as "consideration towards any work carried" u/s 194C of the Act, within the limb of *"consideration towards carriage of goods or passengers by any mode of transport other than by Railways."*

However, it needs to be appreciated that transmission of electricity or wheeling via the transmission system network of a power transmission company is a process and it can't be considered as carriage of goods, simplicitor. Also, treating the transmission system network of the transmission companies, as mode of transportation, will be highly presumptuous.

The Hon'ble Cuttack ITAT, in the case of GRIDCO Ltd vs ACIT 49 SOT 363 had observed as under:

"Further the scope of Section194C was extended by inserting Explanation III by including the specific items within its provision. Accordingly, by inserting Explanation III to section 194c w.e.f. 1.7.1995, the provisions relating to deduction of tax at source has been enlarged by bringing some of the service contracts within the provisions of Section 194C. In a way by

inserting Explanation III the word work in Section 194C has been extended so as to include four types of service contracts within the purview of section 194C. Therefore, Section194C now covers only four types of services beyond what was original enacted i.e., advertising, broadcasting and telecasting including production of programs for such broadcasting or telecasting, carriage of goods and passengers by any mode of transport other than by railways, and catering. Undisputedly the transmission and wheeling charges are not covered in this amendment. Accordingly, it could not be said that transmission charges or wheeling charges require deduction of tax at source u/s.194C of the Act."

CONCLUSION: For the sake of brevity, the above stated comprehensive analysis may be summed up as under:

(i)Transmission & Wheeling Charges can't be considered as Fees for Technical Services u/s 194J of the Income Tax Act as installation & operation of sophisticated equipments with a view to earn income by allowing the users to avail the benefits of such equipments does not tanta-amounts to rendering of "Technical Services" within the meaning of Explanation 2 to section 9(1)(vii) of the Act. Rendering of services by using some sophisticated equipments/ technical systems is different from charging fees for rendering technical services.

The present legal position, in relation to the applicability of TDS on Transmission & Wheeling Charges, u/s 194J of the Act, stands settled and concluded by the dismissal of Special Leave Petition (SLP), of Revenue Authorities, by the Hon'ble Apex Court in SLP(C) No. 853/2016 in the case of CIT (TDS) vs. Delhi Transco Limited, and as such the transmission & wheeling charges, can't be considered as "Fees for Technical Services" so as to attract TDS applicability u/s 194J of the Act.

(ii) Transmission & Wheeling Charges can't be considered as Rent u/s 194I of the Income Tax Act, as if an advantage is taken from sophisticated equipment installed and provided by another, it can't be construed that the recipient/customer uses the equipment as such. The customer merely makes use of the facility, though he does not himself use the equipment. The transmission system networks are owned, controlled, operated and physically possessed by transmission companies, and as such the availment of benefits of the standard facility viz. transmission system network, by power distribution companies, can't be construed as use of such facility so as to attract TDS liability u/s 194I of the Act. There are several judgements of ITAT & High Courts (as mentioned supra), in this regard, so present legal position is also more or less settled in this regards.

(iii) Applicability or Otherwise of TDS on Transmission & Wheeling Charges u/s 194C of the Act: The transmission of electricity via the transmission system network of transmission companies, being a systematic process, ought not to be considered as merely carriage of goods simplicitor and the transmission system network, ought not to be treated as mode of transport, so as to attract TDS liability u/s 194C of the Act.

If Transmission of Electricity is to be considered as "Work in relation to Carriage of Goods" so as to warrant deduction of TDS under section 194C of the Act, then on the same footing, Distribution of Electricity may also have to be considered as "work" so as to require deduction of TDS u/s 194C, from our electricity bills. But this cannot be so. However, at present there are a very few legal precedents in this regard.

TAXALOGUE 15

Commission Agents & Brokers: GST Perspective

"By sharing knowledge about GST Legislative Provisions,
We can do our bit as "Growth Agents" of our Country (Principal)"

Oxford Dictionary defines an *"Agent"* as *"a person who acts on behalf of another person or group."*

The connotation of the word *"Agent"* under the GST Legislature is also on same lines.

Under Erstwhile Service Tax Regime:

The Commission Agent was defined as under:

"Commission Agent" means any person who acts on behalf of another person and causes sale or purchase of goods, or provision or receipt of services, for a consideration, and includes any person who, while acting on behalf of another person -

(i) deals with goods or services or documents of title to such goods or services; or

(ii) collects payment of sale price of such goods or services; or

(iii) guarantees for collection or payment for such goods or services; or

(iv) undertakes any activities relating to such sale or purchase of such goods or services."

The services rendered by Commission Agents were taxable under the Head *"Business Auxiliary Services"* under clause Section 65 (105) (zzb) of the Finance Act, 1994, w.e.f. 01.07.2003 vide Notification No.7/2003- ST dated 20.6.2013.

Under Present GST Regime:

The term "agent" has been defined under sub-section (5) of section 2 of the CGST Act as follows:

"agent" means a person, including a factor, broker, commission agent, arhatia, del credere agent, an auctioneer or any other mercantile agent, by whatever name called, who carries on the business of supply or receipt of goods or services or both on behalf of another.

The following two key elements emerge from the above definition of agent:

a) the term "agent" is defined in terms of the various activities being carried out by the person concerned in the principal-agent relationship; and

b) the supply or receipt of goods or services has to be undertaken by the agent on behalf of the principal.

(I) KEY ASPECTS IN GST LEGISLATION:

(a) GST Registration:

A Commission Agent is required to obtain **Compulsory Registration** u/s 24(vii) of CGST Act, irrespective of its turnover. Thus, the threshold limit of Rs.20 lakh as enunciated in section 22(1) of CGST Act, does not apply to an Agent.

The extract of Section 24 of CGST Act, 2017 is reproduced as under:

Compulsory registration in certain cases.

"Notwithstanding anything contained in sub-section (1) of section 22, the following categories of persons shall be required to be registered under this Act,--
(i).....
....
(vii) persons who make taxable supply of goods or services or both on behalf of other taxable persons whether as an agent or otherwise;

(b) Value of Taxable Supply:

The value of taxable supply rendered by an agent shall include the amount of consideration/commission being received by the agent, for the value of goods/service provided by the agent to his principal. It shall not include the amount of reimbursement claimed by the agent from the principal.

(c) GST Rate, SAC Code & Effective Date of Application:

GST Rate of 18% is applicable on the taxable value of supply provided by the agent.

Bird's Eye View of All Categories of "Commission Agents" under GST Legislature

Description	SAC Code	Rate (%)	Effective From
Services (22)			
Land sales on a fee/**commission** basis or contract basis	997223	18	28-06-2017
Building sales on a fee/**commission** basis or contract basis	997222	18	28-06-2017
Services provided for a fee/**commission** or contract basis on retail trade	996211	18	28-06-2017
Services provided for a fee/**commission** or contract basis on wholesale trade	996111	18	28-06-2017

Property management services on a fee/**commission** basis or contract basis	997221	18	28-06-2017
Real estate appraisal services on a fee/**commission** basis or contract basis	997224	18	28-06-2017
Sale of other advertising space or time (except on **commission**)	998366	18	28-06-2017
Sale of advertising space in print media (except on **commission**)	998363	5	28-06-2017
Purchase or sale of advertising space or time, on **commission**	998362	18	28-06-2017

Description	Code	Rate	Date
Services by way of pure labour contracts of construction, erection, **commission**ing, or installation of original works pertaining to a single residential unit otherwise than as a part of a residential complex.	9954	Nil	28-06-2017
Services provided by way of pure labour contracts of construction, erection, **commission**ing, installation, completion, fitting out, repair, maintenance, renovation, or alteration of a civil structure or any other original works pertaining to the beneficiary-led individual house construction or enhancement under the Housing for All (Urban) Mission or Pradhan Mantri Awas Yojana.	9954	Nil	28-06-2017
Services supplied by electricity distribution utilities by way of construction, erection, **commission**ing, or installation of	99	Nil	27-07-2018

infrastructure for extending electricity distribution network upto the tube well of the farmer or agriculturalist for agricultural use			
Services in wholesale trade. Explanation-This service does not include sale or purchase of goods but includes: Ð Services of **commission** agents, commodity brokers, and auctioneers and all other traders who negotiate whole sale commercial transactions between buyers and sellers, for a fee or **commission** Services of electronic whole sale agents and brokers, Ð Services of whole sale auctioning houses.	9961	18	28-06-2017
Service provided by Fair Price Shops to Central Government by way of sale of wheat, rice and coarse grains under Public Distribution System(PDS) against consideration in the form	9962	Nil	8/22/2017

of **commission** or margin.			
Service provided by Fair Price Shops to Central Government by way of sale of wheat, rice and coarse grains under Public Distribution System(PDS) against consideration in the form of **commission** or margin.	9961	Nil	8/22/2017
Service provided by Fair Price Shops to State Governments or Union territories by way of sale of kerosene, sugar, edible oil, etc. under Public Distribution System (PDS) against consideration in the form of **commission** or margin.	9962	Nil	8/22/2017
Service provided by Fair Price Shops to State Governments or Union territories by way of sale of kerosene, sugar, edible oil, etc. under Public	9961	Nil	8/22/2017

Distribution System (PDS) against consideration in the form of **commission** or margin.			

| Support services to agriculture, forestry, fishing, animal husbandry. Services relating to cultivation of plants and rearing of all life forms of animals, except the rearing of horses, for food, fibre, fuel, raw material or other similar products or agricultural produce by way ofÑ (a) agricultural operations directly related to production of any agricultural produce including cultivation, harvesting, threshing, plant protection or testing; (b) supply of farm labour; (c) processes carried out at an agricultural farm including tending, pruning, cutting, harvesting, drying, cleaning, trimming, sun drying, fumigating, curing, sorting, grading, cooling or bulk packaging and such like operations which do not | 9986 | Nil | 28-06-2017 |

alter the essential characteristics of agricultural produce but make it only marketable for the primary market; (d) renting or leasing of agro machinery or vacant land with or without a structure incidental to its use; (e) loading, unloading, packing, storage or warehousing of agricultural produce; (f) agricultural extension services; (g) services by any Agricultural Produce Marketing Committee or Board or services provided by a **commission** agent for sale or purchase of agricultural produce.

(d) **GST Returns:**

An Agent registered as Normal GST Dealer shall file:
GSTR-3B – monthly;
GSTR-1 – quarterly;
GSTR-2, GSTR-3 - yet to be notified;
GSTR-9 – annually.

(e) **Input Tax Credit:** An Agent can claim the Input Tax Credit on all the Inputs and Input Services used for his business purpose.

(II) Analysis of Applicability of GST on Indenting Agents/Commission Agents rendering services as an "Intermediary" between an exporter abroad receiving such services and an Indian importer.

The term *'Intermediary'* has been defined in Section 2(13) of IGST Act, 2017 as under:-

'intermediary' means a broker, an agent or any other person, by whatever name called, who arranges or facilitates the supply of goods or services or both, or securities, between two or more persons, but does not include a person who supplies such goods or services or both or securities on his own account"

The question of applicability or otherwise of GST on commission received by Indian Indenting/Commission Agents for rendering services as an "Intermediary" between an exporter abroad receiving such services and an Indian importer was the subject matter of consideration in a recent Ruling dated 10/08/2018, of the

Hon'ble AAR in the case of "**Mrs. Vishakhar Prashant Bhave - Micro Instruments** (GST AAR Maharashtra), in Appeal No. GST-ARA-23/2018-19/B-87.

In the said Ruling, the Hon'ble AAR has answered the raised questions as under :

"Question (i) Whether the "Commission" received by the Applicant in convertible Foreign Exchange for rendering services as an "Intermediary" between an exporter abroad receiving such services and an Indian importer of an Equipment, is an "export of service" falling under section 2(6) & outside the purview of section 13 (8) (b), attracting zero-rated tax under section 16 (1) (a) of the Integrated Goods and Services Tax Act, 2017?

Answer :- Answered in the negative.

Question (ii) If the answer to the Q. (i) is in the negative, whether the impugned supply of service forming an integral part of the cross-border sale/purchase of goods, will be treated as an "intra-state supply" under section 8 (1) of the IGST Act read with section 2(65) of the MGST Act attracting CGST/MGST ? And, if so at what Rate?

Answer: The said supply will be treated as Inter-State Supply and not Intra State Supply and IGST will be levied @ 18%."

In answering the above questions, the Hon'ble AAR have observed that the applicant falls in the category of "intermediary" as defined in section 2(13) of IGST Act, 2017 and as the supplier of service, i.e the applicant is located in India and the recipient of service i.e. foreign exporter is located outside India, Section 13 of the IGST Act, 2017 would be applicable to determine the place of service.

The Hon'ble AAR further observed that as per Section 13(8)(b) of the IGST Act, the place of supply of "intermediary services" shall be the location of the supplier of services, in this case, the applicant. Since the place of supply of services in the instant case is in taxable territory of India, the said intermediary services cannot be treated as export of services under the provisions of the GST laws. In order to classify as 'export of service', as per section 2(6) of the Integrated Goods and Service Tax Act, 2017, one of the crucial condition as contained under sub-clause (iii) is that the place of supply of service should be outside India. In the subject case, the place of supply shall be location of the supplier of services i.e. in India and therefore such 'intermediary services' cannot be classified as 'export of services'. In case the intermediary services are provided to the recipient located outside India, the inter-state provisions as contained under section 7(5)(c) shall be applicable and hence IGST is payable under such transaction.

It is pertinent to mention here that Section 13 of IGST Act 2017, contains the provisions concerning the determination of place of supply of services where location of supplier or location of recipient is outside India.

In such cases, as per the default section 13(2) of IGST, the place of supply of services except the services specified in sub-sections (3) to (13) of section 13, shall be the location of the recipient of services, which is outside India.

However, eleven exceptions have been carved out as contained in sub sections (3) to (13) of section 13 of IGST Act, wherein, the location of the supplier of services has been said to be the place of supply. One such exception is that of "intermediary services" as contained in clause (b) of subsection (8) of section 13 of IGST Act.

However, in view of the multiple representations from the stake holders in the Industry, the GST Legislative Authorities are considering to make suitable amendments so as to bring in the "intermediary services" within the purview of default section 13(2) instead of the exception carved out in section 13(8)(b) of IGST Act, so as to enable the consideration of such "intermediary services" being performed by Indian indenting agents to the foreign exporters as "export of services" and as such to bring the said intermediary services from outside the ambit of GST levy.

(III) Scope of Principal-Agent relationship in the context of Schedule I of the CGST Act

In terms of Schedule I of the Central Goods and Services Tax Act, 2017 (the "CGST Act"), the supply of goods by an agent on behalf of the principal without consideration has been deemed to be a supply. In this connection, in order to clarify some of the issues regarding the scope and ambit of the principal-agent relationship under GST, it will be worthwhile to consider the undermentioned legal provisions and their implications.

The term "agent" has been defined under sub-section (5) of section 2 of the CGST Act as follows:
"agent" means a person, including a factor, broker, commission agent, arhatia, del credere agent, an auctioneer or any other mercantile agent, by whatever name called, who carries on the business of supply or receipt of goods or services or both on behalf of another.

As per section 182 of the Indian Contract Act, 1872, an "agent" is a person employed to do any act for another, or to represent another in dealings with third person. The person for whom such act is done, or who is so represented, is called the "principal". As delineated in the definition, an agent can be appointed for performing any act on behalf of the principal which may or may not have the potential for representation on behalf of the principal. So, the crucial element here is the representative character of the agent which enables him to carry out activities on behalf of the principal.

From this, it can be deduced that the crucial component for covering a person within the ambit of the term "agent" under the CGST Act is corresponding to the representative character identified in the definition of "agent" under the Indian Contract Act, 1872.

Further, the two limbs of any supply under GST are "consideration" and "in the course or furtherance of business". Where the consideration is not extant in a transaction, such a transaction does not fall within the ambit of supply. But, in certain scenarios, as elucidated in Schedule I of the CGST Act, the key element of consideration is not required to be present for treating certain activities as supply. One such activity which has been detailed in para 3 of Schedule I (hereinafter referred to as "the said entry") is reproduced hereunder:

3. Supply of goods —
(a) by a principal to his agent where the agent undertakes to supply such goods on behalf of the principal; or
(b) by an agent to his principal where the agent undertakes to receive such goods on behalf of the principal.

Here also, it is worth mentioning that all the activities between the principal and the agent and vice versa do not fall within the scope of the said entry.

Firstly, **the supply of services** between the principal and the agent and vice versa is outside the ambit of the said entry, and would therefore require "consideration" to consider it as supply and thus, be liable to GST.

Secondly, the element identified in the definition of "agent", i.e., "supply or receipt of goods on behalf of the principal" has been retained in this entry.

It may be noted that the crucial factor is how to determine whether the agent is wearing the representative hat and is supplying or receiving goods on behalf of the principal. Since in the commercial world, there are various factors that might influence this relationship, it would be more prudent that an objective criteria is used to determine whether a particular principal-agent relationship falls within the ambit of the said entry or not. Thus, the key ingredient for determining relationship under GST would be whether the invoice for the further supply of goods on behalf of the principal is being issued by the agent or not. Where the invoice for further supply is being issued by the agent in his name then, any provision of goods from the principal to the agent would fall within the fold of the said entry. However, it may be noted that in cases where the invoice is issued by the agent to the customer in the name of the principal, such agent shall not fall within the ambit of Schedule I of the CGST Act. Similarly, where the goods being procured by the agent on behalf of the principal are invoiced in the name of the agent then further provision of the said goods by the agent to the principal would be covered by the said entry. In other words, the crucial point is whether or not the agent has the authority to pass or receive the title of the goods on behalf of the principal.

Looking at the convergence point between the character of the agent under both the CGST Act and the Indian Contract Act, 1872, the following scenarios are discussed, for the sake of better understanding:

Scenario 1

Mr. A appoints Mr. B to procure certain goods from the market. Mr. B identifies various suppliers who can provide the goods as desired by Mr. A, and asks the supplier (Mr. C) to send the goods and issue the invoice directly to Mr. A. In this scenario, Mr. B is only acting as the procurement agent, and has in no way involved himself in the supply or receipt of the goods. Hence, in accordance with the provisions of this Act, Mr. B is not an agent of Mr. A for supply of goods in terms of Schedule I.

Scenario 2

M/s XYZ, a banking company, appoints Mr. B (auctioneer) to auction certain goods. The auctioneer arranges for the auction and identifies the potential bidders. The highest bid is accepted and the goods are sold to the highest bidder by M/s XYZ. The invoice for the supply of the goods is issued by M/s XYZ to the successful bidder. In this scenario, the auctioneer is merely providing the auctioneering services with no role played in the supply of the goods. Even in this scenario, Mr. B is not an agent of M/s XYZ for the supply of goods in terms of Schedule I.

Scenario 3

Mr. A, an artist, appoints M/s B (auctioneer) to auction his painting. M/s B arranges for the auction and identifies the potential bidders. The highest bid is accepted and the painting is sold to the highest bidder. The invoice for the supply of the painting is issued by M/s B on the behalf of Mr. A but in his own name and the painting is delivered to the successful bidder. In this scenario, M/s B is not merely providing auctioneering services, but is also supplying the painting on behalf of Mr. A to the bidder, and has the authority to transfer the title of the painting on behalf of Mr. A. This scenario is covered under Schedule I.

A similar situation can exist in case of supply of goods as well where the C&F agent or commission agent takes possession of the goods from the principal and issues the invoice in his own name. In such cases, the C&F/commission agent is an agent of the principal for the supply of goods in terms of Schedule I. The disclosure or non-disclosure of the name of the principal is immaterial in such situations.

Scenario 4

Mr A sells agricultural produce by utilizing the services of Mr B who is a commission agent as per the Agricultural Produce Marketing Committee Act (APMC Act) of the State. Mr B identifies the buyers and sells the agricultural produce on behalf of Mr. A for which he charges a commission from Mr. A. As per the APMC Act, the commission agent is a person who buys or sells the agricultural produce on behalf of his principal, or facilitates buying and selling of agricultural produce on behalf of his principal and receives, by way of remuneration, a commission or percentage upon the amount involved in such transaction.

In cases where the invoice is issued by Mr. B to the buyer, the former is an agent covered under Schedule I. However, in cases where the invoice is issued directly by Mr. A to the buyer, the commission agent (Mr. B) doesn"t fall under the category of agent covered under Schedule I.

In scenario 1 and scenario 2, Mr. B shall not be liable to obtain registration in terms of clause (vii) of section 24 of the CGST Act. He, however, would be liable for registration if his aggregate turnover of supply of taxable services exceeds the threshold specified in sub-section (1) of section 22 of the CGST Act. In scenario 3, M/s B shall be liable for compulsory registration in terms of the clause (vii) of section 24 of the CGST Act. In respect of commission agents in Scenario 4, notification No. 12/2017 Central Tax (Rate) dated 24.06.2017 has exempted "services by any APMC or board or services provided by the commission agents for sale or purchase of agricultural produce" from GST. Thus, service provided by the commission agent for sale or purchase of agricultural produce is exempted. Such commission agents (even when they qualify as agent under Schedule I) are not liable to be registered according to sub-clause (a) of sub-section (1) of section 23 of the CGST Act, if the supply of the agricultural produce, and /or other goods or services supplied by them are not liable to tax or wholly exempt under GST. However, in cases where the supply of agricultural produce is not exempted and liable to tax, such commission agent shall be liable for compulsory registration under sub-section (vii) of section 24 of the CGST Act.

Source: CBEC Circular No. 57/31/2018-GST, dated the 4th September, 2018

"Change is often the agent of progress in ways we can't always readily see in the early days & GST Reform is one such agent."

TAXALOGUE 16

Is GST Applicable on Naturopathy, Ayurveda, Yoga, Siddha, Unani & Homeopathy Based Medical Treatments?

Recently the Regulatory Body of Indirect Taxes i.e. the Central Board of Indirect Taxes (CBIC), has issued a CBEC Notification No. 12/2017-Central Tax Rate dated 28.6.2017, exempting **"health care services"** rendered at clinical establishments by authorized medical professionals or paramedics, from the applicability of GST, vide entry no. 74, in the said notification.

As per clause 2(zg), "health care services" means any service by way of diagnosis or treatment or care for illness, injury, deformity, abnormality or pregnancy **in any recognised system of medicines in India.**

Following Systems of Medicine are recognized in India:

(i) Allopathy

(ii) Ayurveda

(iii) Siddha

(iv) Unani

(v) Homeopathy

(vi) Yoga

(vii) Naturopathy

Yoga, Naturopathy, Ayurveda, Siddha, Unani and Homeopathy systems of medicine, just like Allopathy, are also duly recognized systems of medicine in India, and as such shall fall in the category of "Health Care Services" so as to qualify for exemption from GST, at par with Allopathy based medical treatments.

It is worthwhile to mention here that by virtue of entry no. 77 of CBEC Notification No. 12/2017-Central Tax Rate, and CBEC Circular No. 32/06/2018-GST, bearing F.No. 354/17/2018-TRU, dated 16.2.2018, the accommodation charges/room rent, retention money, food charges and fees payments being charged from in-patients, by medical institutes/clinical establishments/hospitals, providing health care services as defined under clause 2(zg) of notification No. 12/2017-CT(Rate), have been categorically exempted from the levy of GST.

Naturopathy, Ayurveda & Yoga systems of medicine involve a wholesome therapeutic treatment involving lifestyle changes. Most naturopathy, ayurveda & yoga treatments require accommodation on the part of the patient ranging from 3 days to 3 months, depending on illness and its severity, and as such residential courses are a common feature of such naturopathy, ayurveda & yoga based medical treatments.

As the main purpose and objective of provision of such accommodation facilities to the patients availing the naturopathy, ayurveda & yoga based treatments, rendered by the establishments/institutions/charitable organisations/naturopathy centers, is the medical treatment and accommodation is just an incidental requirement of such treatment, therefore, the entire package of such medical treatments, along with the provision of food and accommodation to the in-patients, shall be considered as composite supply within the meaning of section 2(30) of GST Act, with the exempt services portion i.e. naturopathy/ayurveda/yoga services, as the principal supply & the provision of food and accommodation to the in-patients, as the incidental/secondary supply, and as such the entire package of services shall be considered as outside the purview of the levy of GST, in conformity with the above mentioned entry no. 77 of CBEC Notification No. 12/2017-Central Tax Rate, and CBEC Circular No. 32/06/2018-GST, bearing F.No. 354/17/2018-TRU, dated 16.2.2018.

Conclusion: To sum up, naturopathy, yoga, ayurveda, siddha, unani and homeopathy based systems of medicine, are equally effective, responsive, natural, and wholesome systems of medicine, and are duly recognised systems of medicine in our country, at par with allopathy based system of medicine. Therefore, medical establishments/ institutions/charitable organisations/naturopathy centers, providing medical treatments through such duly recognized systems of medicine, through qualified and approved practitioners, shall be treated at par with the hospitals/medical institutes/clinical establishments providing allopathy based medical treatments and similar exemption of healthcare services and the incidental accommodation and fooding charges from the levy of GST, as available to such hospitals/clinical establishments, shall also be made available to the medical establishments/charitable organisations/naturopathy centers, providing naturopathy, yoga, ayurveda, siddha, unani and homeopathy based medical treatments.

Promotion and development of "Yoga" and "Ayurveda" has been in the forefront priority and focus area of our Government in Centre under our Prime Minister Sh. Narendra Modi ji. Our Government has been successful in making the United Nations declare 21 June as International Yoga Day. Therefore, in line with the Legislative intent and the Government's commitment to bring Yoga, Ayurveda and Naturopathy based treatments at the forefront, it is desirable that the competent authorities and the GST Council, should take due cognizance of the above write-up and shall issue appropriate notification in this regard.

TAXALOGUE 17

GST Rate on Locomotive Engines Used Solely in Indian Railways: An Undying Conundrum!!

REQUIREMENT OF CLARIFICATION IN THE UPCOMING UNION BUDGET 2020/ GST COUNCIL MEET, CONCERNING THE CONTRADICTORY AAR RULING HOLDING ENGINES USED SOLELY IN RAILWAYS, CLASSIFIABLE UNDER CHAPTER 84 ATTRACTING 18% GST AND NOT UNDER CHAPTER 86 ATTRACTING CONCESSIONAL 5% GST

Case Name : Cummins India Limited, In re (GST AAR Maharashtra)
Appeal Number : No. GST-ARA-66/2018-19/B-162
Date of Judgement/Order : 19/12/2018
Courts : AAR Maharashtra (157) Advance Rulings (804)

In this case, the applicant M/s Cummins India Ltd, has raised the undermentioned question before the Hon'ble AAR, for determination viz.

Question: *Whether engine manufactured and supplied solely and principally for use in railways/locomotives are classifiable under HSN Heading 8408 or under HSN Heading 8607 of the Customs Tariff (which has been borrowed for classification purposes under GST regime) as a part used solely or* *principally for Railways or Tramway Locomotives or Rolling Stock?*

Observations & Findings of Hon'ble AAR:

"The applicant has submitted that they are manufacturers of various products one of which are "engines" ('subject engine') manufactured for Railways/Locomotive manufacturers as per the design specifications provided by them and are 'solely and principally' used in railways/locomotive engines. These subject engines have sole use of main propulsion in railways/locomotives and have no alternate usage. The issue before us is whether the subject engines manufactured by applicant are classifiable under heading 8408 as Compression-Ignition Internal Combustion Piston Engines (Diesel or Semi-Diesel Engines) or under heading 8607 as 'Parts of Railways or Tramway Locomotives or Rolling-Stock'.

*The applicant has submitted that the rationale behind introducing GST with varied rate structure, is evident from the fact that entire Chapter 86 which covers in its fold articles such as railways, locomotive, rolling stock and parts thereof which are of substantial significance for public at large is subject to a levy of GST at the rate of 5%. According to them this submission also find force by **Circular No. 30/4/2018-GST dated January 25, 2018** which clarifies that goods supplied to railways, which are classified under Chapter 86 attract GST at the rate of 5%.*

*We find that **Circular No. 30/4/2018-GST dated January 25, 2018** has clarified that only the goods classified under Chapter 86, supplied to the railways attract 5% GST rate with no refund of unutilised input tax credit and other goods [falling* *in any other chapter], would attract the general applicable GST rates to such goods, under the aforesaid notifications, even if **supplied to the railways**. Therefore it is very important to classify subject engines, whether the same falls under Chapters 8408 or 8607.*

Section Note 2(e) of the Section XVII of the Customs Tariff clearly states that the expression "parts" and "parts and accessories", whether or not they are identifiable as for goods of this section, do not apply to the machines or apparatus of heading 8401 to 8479 .... It is very clear from a reading of the said Note 2 (e) that the subject engines which are "Compression-Ignition Internal Combustion Piston Engines ",running on diesel or semi-diesel, cannot be called as parts of goods of Chapter Headings 86 to 88 of the GST Tariff. What this note effectively states is that the subject engines (being compression-ignition internal combustion piston engines), have individual entity and cannot be called as parts of goods falling under Chapters 86 to 88..............

Hence in view of the above discussions we find that the subject engines manufactured and supplied for use in railway, locomotives are classifiable under HSN Heading 8408 and not under Heading 8607 of the Customs Tariff.........

Author's Humble Take on above Ruling:

In order to have proper appreciation of the facts of the case and to have clear understanding of the issue under consideration, it will be desirable and worthwhile to consider the nature, purpose and applicability of the applicable chapter, section and tariff heading under the

Customs Tariff Act and the GST Act, having a direct bearing on the subject matter under consideration.

The classification of goods under the Goods and Services Tax regime is expressly aligned to Chapter/ Heading / Sub-heading / Tariff item under the First Schedule to Customs Tariff Act, 1975 ('Customs Tariff) and warrants reliance on the rules of interpretation and Section/ Chapter/ General Explanatory note thereto, which provide prescription for interpretation of the Customs Tariff (refer to Explanation (iii) & (iv) in the CGST Rate **Notification 1/2017 dated June 28, 2017)**.

It is pertinent to mention here that Customs Tariff Act follows the common classification system, which is popularly called the Harmonized System of Nomenclature (HSN), developed by the World Customs Organization and is used/ accepted world over.

Section XVI of the Customs Tariff Act containing Tariff Headings/ HSN Classification under Chapters 84 & 85, deals, inter alia, with machinery and mechanical appliances. It deals with the general category of machinery and mechanical appliances, attracting a higher rate of GST @ 18%.

Section XVII of the Customs Tariff Act deals with special items like vehicles, aircraft, vessels and associated transport equipments. Chapter 86 coming under this Section deals exclusively with Railway or Tramway Locomotives, rolling stock and parts thereof; Railway or Tramway track, fixtures and fittings and parts thereof, attracting a concessional GST rate of 5%. This Chapter exclusively deals with specific goods relating to Railway, Tramway and parts thereof.

In coming to the conclusion that the engines manufactured by the applicant, although being exclusively and solely used in Indian Railways, were classifiable under Chapter 84 and not Chapter 86 of the Customs Tariff Act, the Hon'ble AAR has relied heavily on
Note 2(e) of Section XVII - Chapter 86 of Customs Tariff Act, which is being reproduced as under:

"2 The expressions "parts" and "parts and accessories" do not apply to the following articles, whether or not they are identifiable as for the goods of this Section:-
(e) Machines and apparatus of heading Nos. 84.01 to 84.79, and parts thereof; articles of heading No. 84.81 or 84.82 and provided they constitute integral parts of engines or motors, articles of heading No. 84.83."

Thus the Hon'ble AAR have interpreted the above Note 2(e) to conclude that the expression parts and parts and accessories do not apply to machines or apparatus of headings 8401 to 8479, or parts thereof and as such, the engine manufactured and supplied for use in railway, locomotives are classifiable under HSN Heading 8408 and not under Heading 8607 of the Customs Tariff.

However, in the said Ruling, somehow this crucial fact has been overlooked that the said Note 2(e) has to be read together in conjunction with the immediately succeeding

Note 3 of Section XVII & Chapter 86 of Customs Tariff Act, which reads as under:

"3. References in Chapters 86 to 88 to 'parts' or accessories do not apply to parts or accessories which are not suitable for use solely or principally with the articles of those Chapters. A part or accessory which answers to a description in two or more of the headings of those Chapters is to be classified under that heading which corresponds to the principal use of that part or accessory."

In relation to Chapter Note 3, HSN heading reads as:
"(B) Criterion of sole or principal use.
(1) Parts and accessories classifiable both in Section XVII and in another Section.

Under Section Note 3, parts and accessories which are not suitable for use solely or principally with the articles of Chapters 86 to 88 are excluded from those Chapters.

So, this Section Note of HSN makes it clear that final classification is determined by its principal use. The effect of Note 3 is therefore that when a part or accessory can fall in one or more other Sections as well as in Section XVII, its final classification is determined by its principal use.

The classification of goods owing to sole and principal usage thereof in view of Section Note 3 is a widely regarded and accepted position of law and the same is also supported by Circular No. 17/ 90-CX.4, dated 9-7-1990 which clarified that gear, gear boxes per se classified under chapter 84 would attract classification under chapter 86 when specifically designed for use with vehicles of Section XVII. It is to be noted here that though the referred clarification was issued under the erstwhile excise regime, but since the excise tariff too was based on HSN as customs tariff is, an interpretation thereunder would squarely apply to present matter also.

Classification of goods owing to its sole and principal usage is supported by a plethora of judicial precedents. In this regard attention is invited to the decision of Hon'ble Tribunal in the case of Hi-tech Industries Limited vs. Commissioner of Customs, Bangalore (2005 (180) ELT 0356]wherein an identical issue in the context of classification of goods on the basis of principal or sole use of the goods was involved. As a matter of fact, the facts of the said case are applicable mutatis mutandis in present factual matrix. the Hon'ble Tribunal While deciding the case in the favour of the assessee relied on the observations of the Commissioner (Appeals) while passing the Order in Appeal as under:

"It is observed that the impugned product imported by the appellants is a web camera. From the technical literature submitted at the time of personal hearing, it is observed that the camera is not an ordinary camera and functions only with the computer and this camera has got very specific functions and it works basically as a part of the computer and cannot function independently on its own. Thus, it is observed that the web camera imported by the appellant is not an ordinary camera and does not function independently. The image can be captured only when it is connected with the computer. Thus, from the above, it can be seen that the product imported by the appellants is not an ordinary camera and therefore will not fall

under chapter 90 as held by the lower authority. The proper classification will be under chapter 84.73 or 84.71. Besides, a perusal of the aforesaid judgment of the Hon'ble Tribunal also clearly indicates that all those items which come along with the computer are to be treated as spares and accessories. Thus, in view of the submissions made by the appellants and in view of the case law referred to by the appellants at the time of personal hearing, it is observed that the proper classification of the product under classification would be under chapter 8473.30 or 84.71 and not under chapter 90 as held by the lower authority. I set aside the order passed by the lower authority and allow the appeal filed by the appellants."

The above decision of the Hon'ble Tribunal has further been affirmed by the Hon'ble Supreme Court in Commissioner vs. Hi-Tech Computers – 2015 (321) E.L.T. A274 (S.C.)

It is also pertinent to mention here that a similar issue came up for consideration before the Hon'ble CESTAT in the case of Bajaj Auto Ltd. v. Collector of Central Excise, Pune, 1994 (74) E.L.T. 599, where the question as to whether the unspecific parts of IC engines used in motor vehicles are parts of motor vehicles or not, came up for consideration.

The Hon'ble CESTAT gave the answer in the affirmative and observed as under:

"These parts of IC engines which were the main parts in the locomotive should also be termed as part of the locomotive and not as IC engines coming under the general category. Central Board of Excise and Customs had to consider the issue as to

whether a radiator assembly supplied to Indian Railways is to be classified under sub-heading 8607.00 or otherwise. The Board observed that product radiator assembly is designed according to the specifications of the Indian Railways and is for use solely and principally with locomotives of Heading 8601 and 8602. It is clarified that the radiator assembly is not to be classified as parts of IC engines under Heading 8409. This understanding of the Central Board of Excise and Customs is discernible from circular No. 16/90 dated 11-6-1990, which still holds good. If radiator assembly manufactured for Railways for being fitted in locomotives is to be classified under Heading 8607, we do not find any justification in the department taking a view that integral parts of IC engines which form locomotive are outside Chapter Heading 86."

Similarly, the Hon'ble CESTAT in the case of "Diesel Components Works vs. Commissioner of Central Excise 2000(70) ECC 277, have also categorically observed and held that the parts of compression-ignition, internal combustion piston engines, captively consumed in reconditioning the diesel locomotives of Zonal Indian Railways, were classifiable under tariff heading 86.07 under Chapter 86 only and not under the general tariff headings of 84 and 85 of Customs Tariff Act.

In the above Ruling, it was an undisputed fact that the engines manufactured by the applicant Cummins were strictly as per the designs provided by the Railways and the subject engines ipso facto were not capable of generic use since the same had been manufactured to cater to a specific design and configuration. Infact the said engines did not have any other buyer and hence, could not be supplied by the applicant otherwise than to railways/locomotive manufacturer for specific railways application.

In view of customized design/ specification, lack of usage other than in railways/locomotive engines, it is evident that said engines were indeed manufactured solely and principally for its usage by the Railways/Locomotive manufacturers as a part of railways/ tramway/ locomotive and hence, qualify the test of Section Note 3 of Section XVII.

In such a case the subject engines merit their classification under chapter 86 as 'parts of railways or tramway locomotives or rolling stock' notwithstanding a probable separate classification under any other chapter of the Customs Tariff.

Concluding Remarks:

The Legislature has strategically and intentionally provided for an altogether separate and independent Chapter 86 in Section XVII of the Customs Tariff Act dealing exclusively with specific goods and parts & accessories used or supplied exclusively in Railways or Tramway Locomotives, rolling stock and parts thereof and considering the Indian Railways as of strategic and national importance and of substantial significance for public at large, a concessional GST rate of 5% (with no ITC) has been provided for goods, parts and accessories used specifically and exclusively in Indian Railways, falling under that chapter.

All the goods and items falling under Chapter 86 in Section XVII of the Customs Tariff Act may be having their respective independent classifications under Chapter 84 or 85 attracting a higher GST rate of 18%, but the very fact of their end usage in Indian Railways, solely and exclusively, entitles them to be classified under Chapter 86 so as to be eligible for a concessional GST rate of 5% (with no ITC).

Any contrary interpretation or conclusion in this regards, will make redundant and defeat the very essence, purpose and Legislative Intent of introducing the separate Chapter 86 in Schedule XVII of the Customs Tariff Act, for goods and parts & accessories, used solely and exclusively in Indian Railways, so as to make them eligible for a concessional GST rate of 5% (with no ITC).

Therefore in view of the above factual propositions and legal precedents, a suitable clarification either by way of an explanation or otherwise is requested to be made in the relevant and applicable provisions of GST Act in the upcoming Union Budget 2019/ upcoming GST Council Meet so as to ensure correct and proper interpretation and application of the same and to do away with any uncertainty or ambiguity in this regards.

TAXALOGUE 18

Is SC Judgement holding Allowances as part of Basic Wages for PF Contribution Contradictory?

"Is the recent SC judgement holding allowances as part of basic wages for the purpose of determination of PF contribution, in contradiction with the stand of the Law makers and implementors?"

In its recent judgement in the case of RPFC vs. Vivekananda Vidyamandir and others & Surya Roshni Ltd & Ors. vs. The State of Madhya Pradesh EPF RPFC and Ors. 2019 LLR 339 (SC), the Hon'ble Supreme Court have held that allowances other than those of the undermentioned types are to be considered as part of the basic wages u/s 2(b) of the EPF & MP Act, 1952, for the purpose of determination of PF Contribution:

- Allowances which are variable in nature;

- Allowances which are linked to any incentive for production resulting in greater output by an employee; or

- Allowances which are not paid across the board to all employees in a particular category; or

- Allowances which are paid especially to those who avail the opportunity.

Accordingly, the allowances like special allowances, conveyance/travelling allowances, education allowances, and other similar allowances in the cases of the respective petitioners, have been held as part of the basic wages, liable for deduction of PF contribution.

In arriving at the conclusion, the Hon'ble Supreme Court have relied upon its earlier judgements in the cases of 'Bridge & Roof Company (India) Ltd' & 'Manipal Academy of Higher Education', wherein it has been categorically held by the Hon'ble Supreme Court that those allowances which are "universally, necessarily and ordinarily paid to all across the board" are to be considered as basic wages, i.e. only those allowances which are paid universally to all the employees in all the establishments, uniformly, across the board, without any discretion, and not just in some establishments on case to case basis, are to be considered as part of basic wages, and not all the allowances.

However, it appears that the present bench of the Hon'ble Supreme Court have interpreted the said expression "universally, necessarily and ordinarily paid to all across the board" in the context of individual establishments only and not in the context of the entire industry as a whole. Thus, in view of the principle of natural justice and fair play and far reaching implications of disturbing the already well settled position in this regard, a review and reconsideration of the said judgement of the Hon'ble Supreme Court is desirable and warranted.

Legislative Provisions as per the Governing EPF & MP Act, 1952

In order to have proper appreciation and understanding of the issue under consideration, it will be desirable and worthwhile to consider and analyse the relevant provisions of the governing EPF & MP Act, 1952, in this regards.

Section 2(b) of the EPF & MP Act, 1952 reads as under:

"Section 2(b) "basic wages" means all emoluments which are earned by an employee while on duty or on leave or on holidays with wages in either case in accordance with the terms of the contract of employment and which are paid or payable in cash to him, but does not include —

(i) the cash value of any food concession;

(ii) any dearness allowance (that is to say, all cash payments by whatever name called paid to an employee on account of a rise in the cost of living), house-rent allowance, overtime allowance, bonus, commission or any other similar allowance payable to the employee in respect of his employment or of work done in such employment;

(iii) any presents made by the employer;"

"Section 6: Contributions and matters which may be provided for in Schemes.

The contribution which shall be paid by the employer to the Fund shall be ten percent. Of the basic wages, dearness allowance and retaining allowance, if any, for the time being payable to each of the employees whether employed by him directly or by or through a contractor, and the employees' contribution shall be equal to the contribution payable by the employer in respect of him and may, if any employee so desires, be an amount exceeding ten percent of his basic wages, dearness allowance and retaining allowance if any, subject to the condition that the employer shall not be under an obligation to pay any contribution over and above his contribution payable under this section:

Provided that in its application to any establishment or class of establishments which the Central Government, after making such inquiry as it deems fit, may, by notification in the Official Gazette specify, this section shall be subject to the modification that for the words "ten percent", at both the places where they occur, the words "12 percent" shall be substituted:

Provided further that where the amount of any contribution payable under this Act involves a fraction of a rupee, the Scheme may provide for rounding off of such fraction to the nearest rupee, half of a rupee, or the quarter of a rupee.

Explanation I – *For the purposes of this section, dearness allowance shall be deemed to include also the cash value of any food concession allowed to the employee.*

Explanation II – *For the purposes of this section, "retaining allowance" means allowance payable for the time being to an employee of any factory or other establishment during any period in which the establishment is not working, for retaining his services."*

Stand of the Law Making Body i.e. Ministry of Labour & Employment & the Regulatory Body EPFO, before the said SC Judgement on this issue:

Circulars, Notifications & RTI Response issued by the Regulatory Body EPFO:

For ready reference, the important and significant circulars and notifications issued by the Regulatory Body CPFC concerning the issue of interpretation of basic wages u/s 2(b) of EPF & MP Act, 1952, for the purpose of determination of provident fund contribution u/s 6 of the Act, having a direct bearing on the subject matter under consideration are discussed here, as under:

(i) Official Response of EPFO - Head Office, Ministry of Labour & Employment, Govt. of India, New Delhi, bearing F.No. C.IV/1(63)10/RTI/948, in October 2010, in response to one RTI :

In its official response to one RTI, the EPFO – Head Office, Ministry of Labour & Employment, Govt. of India, New Delhi, bearing F.No. C.IV/1(63)10/RTI/948, in October 2010, has categorically clarified that the undermentioned allowances are outside the purview of 'basic wages' u/s 2(b) of the Act, and as such don't attract payment of PF contribution, viz.

(a) House Rent Allowance;

(b) Education Allowance;

(c) Conveyance Allowance;

(d) Washing Allowance;

(e) City Allowance;

(f) Leave Travel Allowance;

(g) Night Shift Allowance;

(h) Special Allowance.

It is a matter of fact that the Hon'ble Supreme Court, during the course of appellate pleadings, in the captioned judgement of *"Surya Roshni Ltd. & Ors. vs. The State of Madhya Pradesh EPF RPFC and Ors. 2019 LLR 339 (SC)*, had not been made privy to the above categorical clarification/response to an RTI, by the Regulatory Body EPFO, Ministry of Labour & Employment, Govt. of India, New Delhi, confirming the non-deduction of PF contribution on above allowances by the Establishments. The EPFO was also a party in the said SC judgement and as such it was duty bound to apprise the Hon'ble Supreme Court about its said clarification/response to an RTI.

Therefore, in view of the above categorical clarification, the stand of the Regulatory Body EPFO, Ministry of Labour & Employment, Govt. of India, New Delhi, concerning the non-deduction of PF contribution on above mentioned allowances, has always been very clear and unambiguous, and as such the establishments, not deducting PF contribution on such allowances, can't be considered as defaulters, with retrospective effect after the above SC Judgement.

(ii) Circular C-III/110001/4/3(72)14/Circular/Hqrs./6693 dated 6.8.2014 regarding "Inspection of establishments splitting wages to reduce PF liability."

In the said circular, the regulatory body CPFC, while interpreting the definition of "basic wages" as per section 2(b) of the Act, to include all emoluments which are earned by an employee while on duty but excludes the cash value of food concession, dearness allowance, HRA, overtime allowance, bonus, commission or any other similar allowance payable to the employee and any presents given by the employer to his employees, has apprehended that the employers split the total wages payable to their employees into several allowances in such a way that the said allowances are covered under the category of exclusions provided u/s 2(b) of the Act and thereby encouraging the subterfuge of splitting of wages to reduce the PF liability, upto 50% of total wages.

In order to curb this, CPFC has directed for the inspection of all those establishments where PF contribution has been deducted on fifty percent or less of total wages.

Thus, in the above circular, the regulatory body CPFC has itself acknowledged that deduction of PF contribution on more than 50% of the total wages is a sufficient compliance by the establishments so as to do away with the requirement of their inspection by PF authorities. In other words, the Regulatory Body CPFC has itself acknowledged that the establishments deducting PF contribution on more than 50% of the total wages of their employees are not indulging in any subterfuge of splitting of wages to reduce the PF liability.

(iii) Recent Deliberations between the High-Level Committee comprising participation from the Ministry of Labour & Employment, Govt. of India and the Regulatory Body CPFC:

In very recent deliberations between the Secretary, Ministry of Labour & Employment, Govt. of India & the Regulatory Body EPFO, the new definition of "wages" has been proposed by the Ministry vide its office memo bearing F.No. S-35012/10/2017-SS.II dated 7.2.2018 and comments from all the stakeholders have been invited.

The newly proposed definition of "wages", reads as under:

"Wages" means all remuneration paid or payable in cash to an employee, if the terms of employment, express or implied, were fulfilled, be payable to a person employed in respect of his employment of work in such employment, and includes any, -

- *(a) basic wages,*
- *(b) dearness allowance and*
- *(c) retaining allowance (if any);*

but does not include-

- *(a) any bonus, commission or any similar allowance payable to the employee in respect of his employment of work done in such employment;*
- *(b) house rent allowance;*
- *(c) The value of any house-accommodation, or of the supply of light, water, medical attendance or other amenity or of any service excluded from the computation of wages b a general or special order of the appropriate Government;*

(d) any contribution paid by the employer to any pension of provident fund, and the interest which may have accrued thereon;

(e) any travelling allowance or the value of any travelling concession;

(f) any sum paid to the employed person to defray special expenses entailed on him by the nature of his employment; or

(g) any retrenchment compensation or any gratuity or other retirement benefit payable to the employee or any ex-gratia payment made to him on the termination of employment;

(h) any overtime allowance; and

(i) cash value of any food grains;

Provided that for calculating the wage under this clause, if any payments made by the employer to the employee under clauses (a) to (i) exceeds one half of the all remuneration calculated under this clause, the amount which exceeds such one-half shall be deemed as remuneration and shall accordingly be added to all remuneration under this clause."

Thus, it is duly evident from above that the governing Regulatory Ministry i.e. the Ministry of Labour & Employment has itself proposed the exclusion of travelling allowance and any sum paid to the employed person to defray special expenses entailed on him by the nature of his employment as per clauses (e) and (f) of the newly proposed section 2(b) of the Act, from the purview of 'wages' for the purpose of determination of PF contribution, among other exclusions.

More importantly, the proviso to the newly proposed section is also in complete alignment with the earlier CPFC's circular no. C-III/110001/4/3(72)14/Circular/Hqrs/6693 dated 6.8.2014, as it stipulates a threshold compliance limit of deduction of pf contribution on 50% of the total wages.

The regulatory body EPFO vide its office memo bearing F.No. C-I/1(81)2017/Wages/1801 dated 8.2.2018 has duly accepted the said newly proposed definition of wages for the purpose of determination of PF contribution.

Justification for Non Applicability of the captioned judgement of Hon'ble Supreme Court in the case of *"Surya Roshni Ltd.& Ors. vs. The State of Madhya Pradesh EPF RPFC and Ors. 2019 LLR 339 (SC)*, to the Establishments deducting and contributing PF contribution on more than the 50% of Total Wages:

It is a matter of fact that the Hon'ble Supreme Court, during the course of appellate pleadings, in the captioned judgement of *"Surya Roshni Ltd. & Ors. vs. The State of Madhya Pradesh EPF RPFC and Ors. 2019 LLR 339 (SC)*, had not been made privy to the above CPFC Circular No. bearing F.No. C-I/1(81)2017/Wages/1801 dated 8.2.2018 and the Labour Ministry's office memo bearing F.No. S-35012/10/2017-SS.II dated 7.2.2018 proposing a new definition of "wages" for the purpose of determination of PF contribution, although both the circulars/office memos had been issued before the date of pronouncement of the said judgement by the Hon'ble Supreme Court, i.e. 28.2.2019, and as such the Hon'ble Supreme Court had no occasion, whatsoever, to consider the acceptable stand of the Law Making Body i.e. the Labour Ministry & the Regulatory Body EPFO/CPFC, that the establishments deducting PF contribution on more than 50% of the total wages of their employees are not indulging in any subterfuge of splitting of wages to reduce the PF liability.

Need of the Hour: Avoidance of High Handed Approach by EPFO Deptt & Officers, after the said SC Judgement:

The above RTI Response and Circulars issued by the Governing & Regulatory Bodies viz. the Labour Ministry, the EPFO & the CPFC, makes its duly evident that the stand of these governing and regulatory bodies, concerning the non-deduction of PF contribution on allowances, has always been very clear and unambiguous.

However, unfortunately, the EPFO field officers are resorting to the outright and blatant misuse of the captioned judgement of the Supreme Court, to put undue pressure on Factories, Shops & Establishments for PF collections for meeting out their budgetary targets for improving service records, and even for their vested and malafide interests.

It is a cardinal principal of Law that the Circulars/Notifications issued by the Law Enforcing/Regulatory Bodies are binding on them and they cannot deviate from their own circulars and notifications.

In view of above, it is requested that suitable instructions may be given to the EPFO Deptt and its Officers to avoid the high handed approach especially with the bonafide and genuine Establishments, who are contributing atleast 50% of total wages of their employees as PF contribution with the EPFO, in order to achieve the Governments' objective of "ease of doing business" in real and effective sense.

SO, FRIENDS NEXT TIME YOU ARE IN RECEIPT OF NOTICE U/S 7A OF EPF & MP ACT, 1952, ASKING TO DEPOSIT PF CONTRIBUTION ON EACH AND EVERY ALLOWANCE, PAID BY YOU TO YOUR EMPLOYEES, DON'T SUCCUMB TO THEIR UNLAWFUL PRESSURE TACTICS AND CONFRONT THEM WITH THE ABOVE STATED LEGAL AND FACTUAL PROPOSITIONS...

TAXALOGUE 19

ESI - Chinta se Mukti only till You Receive Notice u/s 45A of The ESI Act 1948.

The preamble to the Employees' State Insurance Act, 1948, reads, *"An Act to provide for certain benefits to employees in case of sickness, maternity and 'employment injury' and to make provision for certain other matters in relation thereto."*

Therefore, the legislative intent of promulgating the ESI Act, 1948 was to enact a social welfare and beneficent legislation with the object of providing benefits to employees in case of sickness, maternity and employment injury and as such, the official tagline of the Employees State Insurance Corporation (ESIC), "Chinta se Mukti", sounds impressive and convincing.

However, the present sorry state of affairs of ESI hospitals is not hidden from anyone. In addition, the present-day tendency of the concerned ESIC authorities has become to put undue pressure on Factories, Shops & Establishments for ESI collections for meeting out their budgetary targets for improving service records.

The vigor, aggressiveness and willingness as shown by the ESIC authorities in collecting the ESI contributions from factories and establishments, in order to fulfill

their budgetary kitty, must also be reflected in their efforts in making available the medical and other benefits, to the ultimate beneficiaries of such ESI contributions.

Unfortunately, the raising of exorbitant and blatant ESI demands u/s 45A of ESI Act, 1948, under the disguise of non-co-operation from the factory or establishment, has become a routine and regular feature, now a days. As per provisions of section 45A of ESI Act, the ESIC authorities are empowered to determine the ESI Contributions, payable in respect of employees of any factory or establishment, based on the records available with them.

Interestingly, presently, many establishments are receiving notices u/s 45A of ESI Act, wherein they are being required to deposit ESI contributions on each and every expenditure incurred by them, be it in the nature of wages or not, and including expenditure incurred on purchase or acquisition of fixed assets including furniture, fixtures and even buildings, on the presumption of presence of labour component, irrespective of whether the recipients/beneficiaries are identifiable or not.

Since ESI Act is a piece of employees' welfare legislation, and as such the definition of an "employee" as per ESI Act, assumes prime significance and infact, it forms the crux of the applicability or otherwise of ESI on any expenditure incurred.

As per section 2(9) of ESI Act, an "employee" means,

"any person employed for wages in or in connection with the work of a factory or establishment to which this Act applies and,

(i) who is directly employed by the principal employer, on any work of, or incidental or preliminary to or connected with the work of, the factory or establishment, whether such work is done by the employee in the factory or establishment or elsewhere; or

(ii) who is employed by or through an immediate employer, on the premises of the factory or establishment or under the supervision of the principal employer or his agent on work which is ordinarily part of the work of the factory or establishment or which is preliminary to the work carried on in or incidental to the purpose of the factory or establishment; or

(iii)

......"

The definition of an "employee" as per provisions of section 2(9) of ESI Act, 1948, is being interpreted to have very wide coverage to include even contractual employees, within its purview. Further, the usage of the expression "any person employed in connection with the work of a factory or establishment to which this Act applies", has also broadened the coverage of ESI legislation, manifolds.

However, the stated broad definition of "employee" in ESI Act, can't be considered as lawful justification for ESIC authorities' blatant and blanket levy of ESI on each and every expenditure being incurred by an establishment.

For the sake of ready reference and clear understanding, it will be worthwhile to consider the well-established & settled legal & factual propositions in relation to the applicability or otherwise of the ESI on different heads of expenditures of an establishment, as under:

(I) Any expenditure incurred in-house by an establishment, can be made subject to the levy of ESI only if it qualifies the definition of "wages" within the meaning of section 2(22) read with section 2(9) of the ESI Act.

(II) Any expenditure which comes within the purview of "wages" but which exceeds the stipulated threshold limit of Rs. 15,000/-, can't be made subject to the levy of ESI.

(III) Any contractual expenditure incurred by an establishment, can be made subject to the levy of ESI only if that establishment assumes the capacity of the "Principal Employer" in relation to the contractual workmen/labour.

(IV) An establishment assumes the capacity of the Principal Employer of the contractual workmen/labour only if it is in a position to supervise & control the work performance of the contractual workmen/staff.

(V) The Independent Contractors having separate registration under the ESI Act must be considered themselves as the Principal Employer of the workmen/labour employed by them in the execution of respective work contracts.

(VI) The ESI legislation is a beneficent piece of social welfare legislation aimed at promoting and securing the well-being of the employees. Thus, the blanket & blind application of ESI provisions on each and every class of contractual payments, where even the beneficiaries/employees are not identifiable or known by the establishment, will defeat the very basis legislative intent of ESI Act.

The application of the aforesaid well settled, legal & factual propositions, to the different expenditure heads of the establishment, will definitely ensure and enable the levy of ESI only on those expenditure heads, on which it is leviable as per provisions of ESI Act.

Further, it will also be appropriate to analyse and discuss the applicability or otherwise of ESI on one very significant and crucial expenditure head, having a direct bearing and relevance on almost all the establishments, viz., expenditure incurred by an establishment on Construction of its Factory/Office Building.

Under this head, a blanket presumption of incurrence of atleast 25% of the total expenditure as wages, is being made by the ESIC authorities, for levying the corresponding ESI on such expenditure.

However, not many know, that the construction site workers were altogether outside the ambit of ESI Scheme, uptill 31.7.2015, by virtue of ESIC Notification No. 4/99 vide Circular No. P-12(11)-11/27/99-Ins. IV dated 14.6.1999.

The relevant operating para of the aforesaid ESIC Notification is reproduced below for ready reference.

"The matter was examined at Hqrs.Office and it is informed that it has been the policy of the ESI Corporation not to cover the workers engaged by the construction agency who belong to unorganized sector due to the peculiar characteristics of the construction industry and the peculiar nature of employment of workers engaged in it. In construction industry the work is carried out through construction workers at the construction sites where the projects are situated. The workers engaged in it are mobile and migratory in nature. The criteria & duration of employment also varies from work to work. Due to the nature of employment and the nature of work place involving the

construction workers, enforcement of ESI Act in respect of such workers and organizing medical and other facilities for them which are normally available under the ESI scheme will be difficult. Therefore the existing scheme under the ESI Act is neither applicable nor suitable for workers engaged in construction sites."

Therefore, the aforesaid ESIC Circular had itself acknowledged that in view of the practical difficulties of organizing medical and other facilities for construction site workers, the ESI scheme is neither applicable nor suitable for such workers.

However, the payments to construction site workers have been brought in the ESI net w.e.f. 1.8.2015 vide ESIC Notification No. P-12/11/11/60/2010-Rev.II, dated 31.7.2015.

It will be interesting to know that now, how it has become possible for the ESIC authorities, to ensure availability of medical and other facilities for construction site workers, in unorganized sector, which previously they were unable to provide.

This itself shows the present mindset of ESIC authorities, of merely acting as collectors of ESI contributions, irrespective of the fact that whether or not the workers, to whom such ESI contributions pertain, will actually benefit, in terms of medical and other facilities.

Otherwise also, the construction works are generally awarded by establishments to big & renowned developers/independent contractors, having independent & separate registration under the ESI Act. Therefore, the respective developers/vendors should be considered as the immediate as well as the principal employer of the workmen/labour employed by them in the execution of the civil works of the establishments and it will not be desirable and justifiable to treat the establishments as their principal employer, for the purpose of levy of ESI.

Reliance in this regards is placed upon the judgment of the Hon'ble Madras High Court in the case of *Dy. Director, Insurance No. V, Employees State Insurance Corporation, Chennai vs. India Pistons Repco Ltd, 2014 LLR (SN) 893:2014(141) FLR (885),* **wherein the Hon'ble Court has categorically held that, the employees of independent contractors could not be held to be the employees of the principal employer for the purpose of payment of contribution under the Employees State Insurance Act, 1948.**

Similar reliance is placed upon the judgment of the jurisdictional **Hon'ble Delhi High Court in the case of** *"Group 4 Securitas Guarding Ltd vs Employees Provident Fund Appellate Tribunal & Ors. WPC No. 4433/2000 & M/s Whirlpool of India Ltd vs Employees*

Provident Fund Appellate Tribunal & Ors. WPC No. 4408/2000 & 4433/2000".

Similarly the Hon'ble Madras High Court in its judgment in the case of *M/S Brakes India Ltd vs Employees Provident Fund Organisation W.P. No. 391 of 2014,* have categorically held that, *"......with respect to the contractors, who are registered with the Provident Fund Department, having independent code number, they are to be treated as independent employer. The petitioner therefore, cannot be treated as "principal employer" for the purposes of these contractors."*

It is pertinent to mention here that the definition of the term "principal employer" as provided in the Employees Provident Fund Act is *"PARI MATERIA"* with that of the "principal employer" in ESI Act & as such the principle ratio that emerges from the aforesaid judgment is clearly applicable on the ESI payments also.

Further, **it is a well-established & settled principle of Law that any establishment confers the status of the principal employer in relation to the contractual workmen/ labour only & only if it is in a position to supervise & control the work performance of the said workmen/labour.**

Reliance in this regards is placed upon the judgment of the **Hon'ble Supreme Court in the case** of *"C.E.S.C. Limited vs Subhash Chandra Bose, 1992 Lab IC 332: AIR*

1992 SC 573", and in the case of "Managing Director, Hassan Co-operative Milk Producers Society Union Ltd vs Asst. Regional Director, Employees State Corporation Ltd, 2010 LLR 561; AIR 2010 SC", wherein the Hon'ble Supreme Court has clearly held that in order to determine the relationship of employer & employee between the principal employer & the employees engaged by the contractor (immediate employer), the supervision or control by the principal employer, over the work performed by the contractual workmen/labour is a sine qua non & a mandatory prerequisite. The Hon'ble Supreme Court has interpreted the expression *"to supervise"* to mean as *"to direct or oversee the performance of operation of any activity & to control its execution.*

The Hon'ble Punjab and Haryana High Court in *Employees State Insurance Corporation v. Malhotra and Co., Chandigarh, (1981 Lab I.C. 475),* has made a distinction between persons employed and persons engaged and the latter are persons engaged for a particular service on whom the employer has no control of supervision or right to take disciplinary action and as such they shall be excluded from ESI.

Similarly, the Hon'ble Kerala High Court in the case of *Regional Director, E.S.I. Corporation v. P. R. Narahari Rao, (1986 Lab I.C. 1981),* has also held that there exists clear distinction between persons engaged and person employed and the former being persons on whom no specific rules of the company is applicable, is not coming under the ESI of the company.

SO, FRIENDS NEXT TIME YOU ARE IN RECEIPT OF NOTICE U/S 45A OF ESI ACT, 1948, ASKING TO DEPOSIT ESI CONTRIBUTION ON EACH AND EVERY EXPENDITURE INCURRED BY YOU IN FURTHERANCE OF YOUR BUSINESS, DON'T SUCCUMB TO THEIR UNLAWFUL PRESSURE TACTICS AND CONFRONT THEM WITH THE ABOVE STATED LEGAL AND FACTUAL PROPOSITIONS...

TAXALOGUE 20

Rationalisation of IBC: A Lot Has Been Done...
Still A Lot More Needs to be Done...

The intent of the Legislature in repealing the erstwhile SICA Act and its substitution with the new Insolvency & Bankruptcy Code (IBC) 2016 was to ensure more effective, sensitive, holistic and timely financial revival of the stressed companies as well as protecting the interests of all stakeholders and financial and operational creditors.

However, three years down the line, faced with several practical and procedural bottlenecks, the IBC 2016 is still improving and evolving and the recent amendments in IBC Amendment Act 2019, as approved by the Union Cabinet are in this direction only and are aimed at bridging the gaps between theoretical idolism and practical implementation.

The recent amendments in IBC Amendment Act 2019 are discussed as under:

(i) Deadline of 360 days including litigation period for Completion of Resolution Plans:

The existing IBC 2016 provides for a time period of 270 days for completion of resolution plans but this time period excludes the time spent in litigations, and judicial process and as such in practical terms this deadline of 270 days was turning out to be redundant and meaningless in view of the prolonged litigation period. So, with a view to make the stipulated deadline for completion of resolution plans effective and meaningful, the proposed amendment provides for the deadline of 360 days inclusive of the litigation period, for completion of the resolution plan.

(ii) Enhancement in Powers of Committee of Creditors (CoC):

The proposed amendment in IBC Amendment Bill 2019 provides the much needed flexibility to the CoC to decide on the distribution of claims on the basis of commercial consideration within the broad framework of mandatory order of priority as stipulated in section 53 of IBC 2016.

(iii) Supremacy of Financial Creditors over Operational Creditors:

In a recent resolution plan in Essar Steel Case, NCALT had treated financial creditors (banks and other secured creditors) to be at par with operational creditors (vendors) in distribution of their respective claims and the said resolution plan has been challenged by the concerned financial creditors in the Supreme Court.

The proposed amendment in IBC Amendment Bill 2019, reiterates and reinforces the supremacy of financial creditors over operational creditors, and simultaneous guarantee of a minimum liquidation value to the operational creditors.

(iv) Majoritarian Criteria of 50% or more for Voting among a particular class of creditors:

The proposed amendment in IBC Amendment Bill 2019 provides that a majority vote of 50% or more from a particular class of creditors will be counted as 100% vote in favour of or against a resolution plan by that particular class of creditors in place of the existing criteria of minimum 66% votes.

(v) Binding Nature of Resolution Plans under IBC:

In line with the recent judgement of the Hon'ble Supreme Court in the case of PCIT vs. Monnet Ispat and Energy Ltd upholding the overriding nature and supremacy of the provisions of the IBC Code 2016 over any other enactment in case of conflicting provisions, by virtue of a non obstante section 238 of IBC Code 2016, the proposed amendment in IBC Amendment Bill 2019, provides that the bankruptcy resolution or liquidation arrived at under IBC shall be binding on central, state and local governments including the income tax and other similar tax authorities.

(vi) **Recognition of Mergers, Demergers and Amalgamations as alternative parts of Resolution Plans under IBC:**

The proposed amendment in IBC Amendment Bill 2019, provides for the inclusion of alternative restricting schemes such as mergers, demergers and amalgamations as part of the resolution plan. At present, the IBC stipulates either rehabilitation/revival of the stressed company as a going concern or its liquidation and does not provide for any other alternative restructuring schemes such as mergers, demergers and amalgamations as part of resolution plan.

All the above proposed amendments are really a very positive and welcome initiatives aimed at ensuring more flexibility, viability, effectiveness and faster implementation of resolution plans under IBC and in reducing the unnecessary litigations and to bring in the much needed stability and certainty in the IBC resolution process.

However, in addition to above, some very crucial and essential reforms and rationalisation measures are also required to be further incorporated in the IBC Act to incentivize and boost the potential buyers/bidders to encourage them to come out with effective resolution plans under IBC. These much needed and desirable reforms in the IBC are discussed as under:

(i) Suitable Amendments in IBC Amendment Act 2019 to ensure Non-Applicability of the MAT provisions u/s 115JB and taxability under sections 28(iv) & 41(1) of the Income Tax Act on the waiver of loans/liabilities of the stressed/insolvent companies under IBC:

The waiver of loans and liabilities of the stressed/insolvent companies by the financial and operational creditors form an integral and crucial part of all the resolution plans aimed at financial revival of insolvent companies under IBC.

The erstwhile SICA expressly contained a provision stipulating the non-applicability of MAT u/s 115JB of the Income Tax Act to the stressed companies under IBC. However, at present there is no such provision in the existing IBC Act.

So with a view to make the resolution plans practically viable and to do away with the possibility of perishing of the resolution proceeds as unwarranted income tax outflows on account of consideration of waiver of loans and liabilities of stressed companies as notional book profits u/s 115JB of the Income Tax Act, it is indeed the need of the hour to incorporate suitable amendments in the IBC Amendment Bill 2019 to ensure non-inclusion of such waiver of loans and liabilities in book profits of stressed/insolvent companies under IBC, for the purpose of MAT determination under MAT provision u/s 115JB of Income Tax Act.

Further, recently the Hon'ble Supreme Court in the case of Mahindra and Mahindra Ltd. [2018] 93 taxmann.com 32 (SC), has laid down the law that waiver of loan shall not be taxable either u/s 28(iv) or s.41(1).

The Apex court has now clarified that 'waiver of loan' should be treated as 'receipt of money' and hence such receipt of money would fall outside the purview of s.28(iv) and accordingly cannot be taxable.

The Apex Court has also held that 'waiver of loan' does not amount to cessation of trading liability and as such the same would not fall within the purview of s.41(1).

Therefore, in view of the binding nature of the above judgement of the Hon'ble Supreme Court and more importantly in order to provide the much needed boost and push to resolution plans under IBC aimed at ensuring financial revival of stressed/insolvent companies, suitable amendments are desirable in the IBC Amendment Bill 2019, so as to ensure the non-applicability of sections 28(iv) and 41(1) of the Income Tax Act on the waiver of loans and liabilities both on capital and revenue accounts, of stressed/insolvent companies in resolution plans under IBC.

(ii) Suitable Amendments in IBC Amendment Act 2019 to ensure Non-Applicability of the provisions of section 56(2)(x) & 50CA of the Income Tax Act to the stressed/insolvent companies whose resolution plans

for their revival have been approved by NCLT under IBC Act:

At present, the potential buyers/bidders desirous of reviving/acquiring stressed/insolvent companies under IBC, face the pressures and litigations from income-tax authorities challenging the valuation aspects of the acquisitions under section 50CA and 56(2)(x) of the Income Tax Act.

Under Sections 50CA and 56(2)(x) of the Income Tax Act, the differential value between the fair market value and the bidding consideration is taxable if the bidding consideration is lower than the fair market value. Section 50CA imposes a tax on this notional capital gain income on the seller and section 56(2)(x) imposes a tax on the buyer by treating the difference as income from other sources.

The FMV of the bidding consideration has to be calculated as per the Rule 11UA of the Income Tax Rules, 1962 with intrinsic book values or listed stock market prices to be taken into account. There may be situations, where the bid price of the securities forming part of resolution plan is lower than the FMV determined under Rule 11UA. Since these transactions of bidding are being undertaken in the open market through a competitive bidding process, it would be grossly unfair to tax the sellers and buyers on this notional income.

Thus, in order to ensure the successful and meaningful implementation of resolution plans under IBC, suitable amendments are desirable in the IBC Amendment Act 2019, so as to ensure the non-applicability of sections 56(2)(x) & 50CA on such stressed/insolvent companies whose resolution plans for their financial revival have been approved by NCLT under IBC.

(iii) **Suitable Amendments in IBC Amendment Act 2019 to ensure Non-Applicability of the provisions of sections 2(1B), 2(19AA) & 72A of the Income Tax Act concerning allowability of carry forward and setoff of losses and unabsorbed depreciation in case of stressed/insolvent companies under IBC Act 2016:**

In making strategic acquisitions of insolvent companies under IBC, the consideration of income tax benefit of availment of set-off benefit towards brought-forward business losses and unabsorbed depreciation of insolvent companies plays a very significant role in luring the potential bidders/buyers and it is a universal phenomenon in almost all strategic and financial revival plans under IBC.

The conditions for availing the benefit of set-off towards brought-forward business losses and unabsorbed depreciation of the amalgamating/demerging entity are stipulated in section 72A of the Act within the meaning of section 2(1B) or 2(19AA) of the Act.

The primary conditions as envisaged in section 72A are that atleast 75% of the shareholders of the amalgamating/demerging entity must be given shareholding in the amalgamated/demerged entity, amalgamated/demerged company must hold at least 75% of the book value of fixed assets of the amalgamating/demerging entity for a minimum period of five years from the date of amalgamation/demerger; and that the new entity must continue the business of the stressed company for a minimum period of five years from the date of amalgamation/demerger. If either of the conditions is not met, the tax benefit of loss and depreciation is to be taxed in the year the condition is breached.

All these conditions, may in a certain type of resolution plans, be difficult to comply with. Plans which require significant divestment of fixed assets for reasons of business viability may be hit by this embargo. The limitation on the continuation of the old business after amalgamation hampers the flexibility of the acquirer to bring about a turnaround by restructuring the old business into a new business which is viable. In such situations, acquirers/bidders would be hampered by not being able to take the amalgamation route.

In view of above, suitable amendments in IBC Amendment Act 2019 are desirable in order to ensure Non-Applicability of the provisions of sections 2(1B),

2(19AA) & 72A of the Income Tax Act concerning allowability of carry forward and setoff of losses and unabsorbed depreciation in case of stressed/insolvent companies under IBC, so as to encourage more potential buyers and bidders to participate in the resolution plans for ensuring the financial revival of such stressed/insolvent companies.

Concluding Remarks:

The government has identified the success of IBC as a key determinant of our country's economic growth, and as such it is imperative for the concerned finance ministry and revenue authorities to have a more compassionate, pragmatic and rational view concerning the above mentioned desirable reforms and rationalisation measures in the IBC Amendment Act 2019 so as to ensure more flexibility, viability, effectiveness and faster implementation of resolution plans under IBC and to reduce the unnecessary litigations and to bring in the much needed stability and certainty in the IBC resolution process.

"Even perfection has room for improvement."
- Ty Warner

TAXALOGUE 21

NBFCs: Impact Assessment of Carrot & Stick Approach of Amendments in Union Budget 2019-20

Non-Banking Financial Companies (NBFCs), often referred to as the "shadow banking system" are playing an increasingly important role in our country's financial systems and their growing influence on our nation's economy is clearly visible in the Union Budget 2019-20 also as a lot of amendments and rationalisation measures concerning NBFCs have been incorporated in the Union Budget.

One of the 'चौपायी' (prose) in "the sacred Sunderkand reads as "भय बिनू होयी ना प्रीति", which means, "without fear there is no respect and love." When Lord Rama's polite request to the Sea to give way to Lanka didn't work, his threat to dry the Sea worked.

The carrot and stick approach always work well in almost all spheres of life and the amendments/rationalisation measures concerning NBFCs in the Union Budget 2019-20, also revolve around this approach only.

(A) CARROTS:

The Union Budget 2019-20 has made several amendments/rationalisation measures aimed at encouraging and incentivizing NBFCs and these are discussed as under:

(I) Amendments in Income Tax Act:

The Hon'ble Finance Minister Smt. Nirmala Sitharaman in her budget speech has stated,

"Incentives to certain Non-banking Financial Companies (NBFCs):

"Non-banking financial companies play an increasingly important role in India's financial system. With the enhanced levels of regulation they are subjected to by the Reserve Bank of India, there is a need to provide greater parity in their tax treatment vis-à-vis scheduled banks. Currently, interest on certain bad or doubtful debts made by scheduled banks and other financial institutions is allowed to be offered to tax in the year in which this interest is actually received. I propose to extend this facility to deposit taking as well as systemically important non-deposit taking NBFCs also."

Presently, interest income on bad or doubtful debts made by NBFCs is charged to tax on accrual basis. However, in cases of scheduled banks, public financial institutions, state financial corporations, state industrial investment corporations, cooperative banks and certain public companies like housing finance companies, interest on bad or doubtful debts is charged to tax on receipt basis. To provide a level playing field, it is proposed that interest on bad or doubtful debts in the case of deposit-taking NBFC and systemically important non deposit-taking NBFC shall be charged to tax on receipt basis. It is also proposed to provide that deduction of such interest shall be allowed to the payer on actual payment."

The existing provisions of section 43D of the Act, inter-alia provides that interest income in relation to certain categories of bad or doubtful debts received by certain institutions or banks or corporations or companies, shall be chargeable to tax in the previous year in which it is credited to its profit and loss account actually received, whichever is earlier. This provision is an exception to the accrual system of accounting which is regularly followed by such assesses for computation of total income. The benefit of this provision is presently available to public financial institutions, scheduled banks, cooperative banks, State financial corporations, State industrial investment corporations and public companies like housing finance companies. With a view to provide a level playing field to certain categories of NBFCs who are adequately regulated, it is proposed to amend section 43D of the Act so as to include deposit-taking NBFCs and systemically important non deposit-taking NBFCs within the scope of this section. Consequentially, as per matching principle in taxation, it is proposed to amend section 43B of the Act to provide that any sum payable by the assessee as interest on any loan or advances from a deposit-taking NBFCs and systemically important non deposit-taking NBFCs shall be allowed as deduction if it is actually paid on or before the due date of furnishing the return of income of the relevant previous year.

Further the newly inserted Explanation 4 to section 43B of the Income Tax Act, provides as under:

"non-banking financial company" shall have the meaning assigned to it in clause (*f*) of section 45-I of the Reserve Bank of India Act, 1934;

'(*e*) "deposit taking non-banking financial company" means a non-banking financial company which is accepting or holding public deposits and is registered with the Reserve Bank of India under the provisions of the Reserve Bank of India Act, 1934;

(*g*) "systemically important non-deposit taking non-banking financial company" means a non-banking financial company which is not accepting or holding public deposits and having total assets of not less than five hundred crore rupees as per the last audited balance sheet and is registered with the Reserve Bank of India under the provisions of the Reserve Bank of India Act, 1934.'.

These amendments will take effect from 1st April, 2020 and will, accordingly, apply in relation to the assessment year 2020-21 and subsequent years.

The said amendments are indeed a welcome and positive initiative of the Government and will ensure the granting of a level playing field to the NBFCs and will also provide the much-needed parity in their tax treatment of interest income vis-à-vis scheduled banks and other financial institutions.

(II) Amendments in the Reserve Bank of India (RBI) Act, 1934:

The enacted rationalisation measures concerning NBFCs also include insertion of a new section 45MBA in the RBI Act, 1934, enabling RBI to consider resolution of financially-troubled NBFCs through a merger or by splitting them into viable and non-viable units called bridge institutions.

For the sake of ready reference, the newly inserted specific section is being reproduced as under:

"Resolution of non-banking financial company

45MBA. (1) Without prejudice to any other provision of this Act or any other law for the time being in force, the Bank may, if it is satisfied, upon an inspection of the Books of a non-banking financial company that it is in the public interest or in the interest of financial stability so to do for enabling the continuance of the activities critical to the functioning of the financial system, frame schemes which may provide for any one or more of the following, namely:--
(a) amalgamation with any other non-banking institution;
(b) reconstruction of the non-banking financial company;
(c) splitting the non-banking financial company into different units or institutions and vesting viable and non-viable businesses in separate units or institutions to preserve the continuity of the activities of that non-banking financial company that are critical to the functioning of the financial system and for such purpose establish institutions called "Bridge Institutions".
Explanation.--For the purposes of this sub-section, "Bridge Institutions" mean temporary institutional arrangement made under the scheme referred to in this sub-section, to preserve the continuity of the activities of a non-banking financial company that are critical to the functioning of the financial system."

(III) Rationalisation Measures in Financial Sector:

(i) Recognising the significant role of NBFCs in sustaining consumption demand as well as capital formation in small and medium industrial segment, a need for the continuous funding of fundamentally sound NBFCs, from banks and mutual funds, without making them unduly risk averse, has been felt and emphasised and accordingly appropriate proposals have been placed in the Union Budget. For purchase of high-rated pooled assets of financially sound NBFCs, amounting to a total of one lakh crore rupees, during the current financial year, Government will provide one time six months' partial credit guarantee to Public Sector Banks for first loss of up to 10%.

(ii) NBFCs which do public placement of debt have to maintain a Debenture Redemption Reserve (DRR) and in addition, a special reserve as required by RBI, has also to be maintained. To allow NBFCs to raise funds in public issues, the requirement of creating a DRR, which is currently applicable for only public issues as private placements are exempt, will be done away with.

(B) STICKS:

As a balancing measure, the Union Budget 2019-20 has also made several amendments aimed at tightening the loose ends in order to ensure better and effective regulatory control over NBFCs, and these are discussed as under:

(I) Amendments in the Reserve Bank of India (RBI) Act, 1934:

Appropriate proposals for strengthening the regulatory authority of RBI over NBFCs are being placed in the Finance (No. 2) Bill. The proposed amendments in the RBI Act, 1934, provides for empowering the RBI to supersede the board of NBFCs (other than those owned by the government). The proposed amendments also authorize the RBI to remove the auditors of NBFC, and call for an audit of any group company of an NBFC, and have a say in the compensation of senior management.

For the sake of ready reference and better understanding, the specific amendments in the RBI Act, 1934 as proposed in the Union Budget 2019-20 are being reproduced as under:

Power of bank (read RBI) *to Remove Directors* (of NBFC) *from office*

"45-ID.(1) Where the Bank is satisfied that in the public interest or to prevent the affairs of a nonbanking financial company being conducted in a manner detrimental to the interest of the depositors or creditors, or financial stability or for securing the proper management of such company, it is necessary so to do, the Bank may, by order and for reasons to be recorded in writing, remove from office, a director (by whatever name called) of such company, other than Government owned nonbanking financial company with effect from such date as may be specified in the said order.

......

(3) Where any order is made in respect of a director of a company under sub-section (1), he shall cease to be a director

of that non-banking financial company and shall not, in any way, whether directly or indirectly, be concerned with, or take part in the management of any non-banking financial company for such period not exceeding five years at a time as may be specified in the order.

(4) Where an order under sub-section (1) has been made, the Bank may, by order in writing, appoint a suitable person in place of the director, who has been so removed from his office, with effect from such date as may be specified in such order."

Supersession of Board of directors of non-banking financial company (other than Government Company).

45-IE. *(1) Where the Bank is satisfied that in the public interest or to prevent the affairs of a non-banking financial company being conducted in a manner detrimental to the interest of the depositors or creditors, or of the non-banking financial company (other than Government Company), or for securing the proper management of such company or for financial stability, it is necessary so to do, the Bank may, for reasons to be recorded in writing, by order, supersede the Board of Directors of such company for a period not exceeding five years as may be specified in the order, which may be extended from time to time, so, however, that the total period shall not exceed five years."*

Power to take action against auditors

"45MAA. Where any auditor fails to comply with any direction given or order made by the Bank under section 45MA, the Bank, may, if satisfied, remove or debar the auditor from exercising the duties as auditor of any of the Bank regulated entities for a maximum period of three years, at a time.".

Power in respect of group companies

"45NAA. (1) The Bank may, at any time, direct a non-banking financial company to annex to its financial statements or furnish separately, within such time and at such intervals as may be specified by the Bank, such statements and information relating to the business or affairs of any group company of the non-banking financial company as the Bank may consider necessary or expedient to obtain for the purposes of this Act.

(2) Notwithstanding anything to the contrary contained in the Companies Act, 2013, the Bank may, at any time, cause an inspection or audit to be made of any group company of a non-banking financial company and its books of account.

Explanation.--For the purposes of this section,--

(a) "group company" shall mean an arrangement involving two or more entities related to each other through any of the following relationships, namely:--

(i) subsidiary – parent (as may be notified by the Bank in accordance with Accounting Standards);

(ii) joint venture (as may be notified by the Bank in accordance with Accounting Standards);

(iii) associate (as may be notified by the Bank in accordance with Accounting Standards);

(iv) promoter-promotee (under the Securities and Exchange Board of India Act, 1992 or the rules or regulations made thereunder for listed companies);

(v) related party;

(vi) common brand name (that is usage of a registered brand name of an entity by another entity for business purposes); and

(vii) investment in equity shares of twenty per cent and above in the entity;

(b) "Accounting Standards" means the Accounting Standards notified by the Central Government under section 133, read *with section 469 of the Companies Act, 2013 and subsection (1) of section 210A of the Companies Act, 1956.".*

(C) Analysis of Present Disciplinary and Regulatory Action of RBI concerning Cancellation of Licenses of NBFCs post Infrastructure Leasing and Financial Services Ltd (IL&FS) Crisis:

Considering the pivotal role of NBFCs as the "shadow banking sector", these have always been considerately and liberally regulated by the Regulator RBI.

However, the surfacing of the Infrastructure Leasing and Financial Services Ltd (IL&FS) Crisis in September 2018, has compelled RBI to tighten the loose ends and to heighten the scrutiny and monitoring of the asset-liability and risk management framework of the NBFCs.

The crisis unfolded when IL&FS defaulted on debt loan repayments of Rs 1,000-crores, resulting in drying up of liquidity in the sector.

Stepping up and tightening its supervision and regulatory control over NBFCs, the RBI has cancelled the registration of total 5048 NBFCs, uptill 31.3.2019 as per RBI's official website. These included NBFCs that failed to meet prudential and capital adequacy norms and also those that voluntarily surrendered registration.

Over half of the cancelled NBFC licenses are attributable to shortfall in Net Owned Funds (NOFs) of NBFCs. At present, the threshold amount that has to be maintained as NOF by NBFCs is stipulated at Rs. 2 crores. The failure to maintain this threshold NOFs of Rs. 2 crores by 31.3.2017 had led to this spurge of license cancellations in 2018 and 2019, post IL&FS crisis.

Previously, since 9.1.1997 when the RBI (Amendment) Act, 1997 came into existence, the requirement in relation to the threshold limit of NOFs of NBFCs was confined to Rs. 25 lakhs only.

Further, by virtue of the provisions of section 45IA(3) of RBI Act, the then existing NBFCs, whose net owned funds (NOFs) were less than twenty-five lakh of rupees as on 09.01.1997, were allowed to continue their business for a period of three years from such commencement. Thereafter, at the request of the NBFCs, the RBI may extend the time by recording reasons in writing. However, such extension of time should not exceed six years in aggregate.

The above requirement of having the minimum net owned fund of twenty-five lakh rupees was enhanced to Rs. 200 lakhs rupees vide RBI Notification No. DNBR.007/CGM(CDS)-2015, dated 27.03.2015.

The RBI, by notification No.DNBR.007/CGM(CDS)-2015, dated 27.03.2015, specified two hundred lakhs rupees as the NOF required for an NBFC to commence or carry on the business. It further provided that an NBFC holding a Certificate of Registration (CoR) and having NOF of less than two hundred lakhs of rupees may continue to carry on the business, if such company achieves the NOF of one hundred lakhs or rupees before 01.04.2016 and two hundred lakhs of rupees before 01.04.2017.

It is a trite law that no notification or circular can override the legislative provisions of the Governing Act.

Therefore, when the Governing Act i.e. the RBI (Amendment) Act 1997, by virtue of the provisions contained in proviso to sub section (3) of section 45IA, itself stipulates the granting of a maximum time period of 6 years for the NBFCs to enhance their net owned funds by giving them sufficient time to continue to carry on the business and comply with the requirements of increased threshold of NOF, then the RBI's subsequent Notification No. DNBR.007/CGM(CDS)-2015, dated 27.03.2015 fixing the cut off deadline for compliance in relation to the requirement of having the enhanced minimum net owned funds of Rs. 200 lakhs, as 1.4.2017, i.e. less than the stipulated maximum time period of 6 years, being in contradiction to the categorical legislative provisions in the Governing Act, needs a review and reconsideration.

Therefore, in relation to the amended requirement of RBI's Notification No. DNBR.007/CGM(CDS)-2015, dated 27.03.2015 of having the enhanced minimum net owned funds of Rs. 200 lakhs in place of the originally envisaged Rs. 25 lakhs, the stipulation of the granting of the maximum time period of 6 years for the NBFCs to comply with the requirement of having the enhanced minimum net owned funds as envisaged in proviso to section 45IA(3) of the RBI (Amendment) Act 1997, has to be read from the date of issue of the said RBI Notification, i.e. from 27.3.2015.

Thus the maximum time period which ought to be granted to NBFC's to comply with the requirement of having the enhanced net owned funds of Rs. 200 lakhs ought to be considered as 6 years from the date of issue of RBI Notification No. DNBR.007/CGM(CDS)-2015, dated 27.03.2015, i.e uptill 27.3.2021 and not 31.3.2017 as has been stipulated in the said notification.

In this regards, reliance can be placed upon the recent judgement of the Hon'ble Madras High Court dated 29-1-2019, in the Consolidated Group of Cases of :

M/s. Nahar Finance and Leasing Limited & M/s.Lodha Finance India Limited & Valluvar Development Finance Pvt Ltd., & M/s.Senthil Finance Private Limited Vs. The Regional Director, Reserve Bank of India,.

The Hon'ble Madras High Court, in its said judgement have held the cancellation of licenses of NBFCs by RBI on account of non-fulfillment of the stipulated threshold criteria of NOF of Rs. 2 crores uptill 31.3.2017, as unlawful and have categorically held that a time period of three years further extendable to 6 years from the date of issue of notification no. DNBR.007/CGM(CDS)-2015, dated 27.03.2015, ought to be granted to NBFCs to enable them to fulfil the said criteria.

It is pertinent to mention here that an amendment concerning the requirement of minimum NOFs of NBFCs has been proposed in the Finance Bill (No. 2), 2019 by clause no. 136 of the Finance Bill, wherein, it has been provided as under:

"136. In the Reserve Bank of India Act, 1934, in section 45-IA, in sub-section (1), for clause (b), the following shall be substituted, namely: —

"(b) having the net owned fund of twenty-five lakh rupees or such other amount, not exceeding hundred crore rupees, as the Bank may, by notification in the Official Gazette, specify:

Provided that the Bank may notify different amounts of net owned fund for different categories of non-banking financial companies."

However, it is duly evident that no amendment has been made in subsection (3) of section 45IA of the RBI Act and as such the proposed amendment will also not make any difference in the legal position as laid down by the Hon'ble Madras High Court in its judgement (as mentioned supra).

Further, the first proviso to Section 45-IA(6) of RBI Act, specifically stipulates that before the cancellation of the CoR on the ground that the NBFC has failed to comply with the provisions of clause (ii) of sub-section (6) of section 45IA of RBI Act, concerning the requirement of having minimum net owned funds, the NBFC shall be given an opportunity on such terms as the RBI may specify for taking necessary steps to comply with such provision or fulfillment of condition. The second proviso provides for a mandatory reasonable opportunity of being heard to be given to NBFC.

However, it was observed by the Hon'ble Madras High Court that CoR of NBFCs were cancelled by the Regulator, without giving them suitable opportunity for taking necessary steps to comply with the requirement of having minimum NOFs and also without granting them proper opportunity of being heard as stipulated in first and second provisos respectively, of section 45IA(6) of the RBI Act, 1934.

Concluding Remarks:
The casual, lethargic and undue liberal regulatory framework over NBFCs, before the IL&FS crisis and the arbitrary, adhoc, knee-jerk and reactive regulatory framework, post the IL&FS crisis, both are undesirable and unjustified. Instead a balanced, pragmatic, consistent, prudent and effective regulatory framework over NBFCs is the need of the hour, in order to ensure the success and growth of this shadow banking sector.

"Before embarking upon any new destination, it is wise and prudent to look back at the footprints of the journey made so far...."

Acknowledgement

Any good piece of 'book-writing-work' not only requires the skills, passion, dedication and perseverance of the author but also involves the selfless and invaluable contribution of many others who are directly or indirectly connected with him/her.

In my case also, this present piece of 'book-writing-work' has become possible and has seen the light of the day only because of the selfless contribution and invaluable support, guidance and blessings of some very dear and special people in my life.

My 'soul-mate - my wife Sonia' and 'my soul - my little son Dhruv' are the first ones who deserve every bit of my gratitude, love, affection and acknowledgement and I owe to them every single second of my personal time which I spent on penning down this piece of writing and not with them. It was their patience, encouragement, unconditional love and invaluable support that motivated me and allowed me to go ahead with this noble pursuit.

I also owe my sincere gratitude to my Parents who have always selflessly and lovingly showered and blessed me with all their love, support and guidance through-out.

I also owe my sincere gratitude, respect and acknowledgement to the Amazon Kindle Direct Publication (KDP), for giving me such a nice and reputed platform to showcase my writing skills.

Most importantly, I thank and pray the Almighty who have always blessed me with physical and mental well-being and have always shown me the right path in my life.

*With Warm Regards
Mayank Mohanka*

www.ingramcontent.com/pod-product-compliance
Lightning Source LLC
Chambersburg PA
CBHW020729180526
45163CB00001B/164